THE RIGHT TO BE YOU

NANCY PAUL

Cartoons by Joanna Bowers

Chartwell-Bratt
Studentlitteratur

© Nancy Paul and Chartwell Bratt Ltd, 1985

Chartwell-Bratt (Publishing and Training) Ltd
ISBN 0-86238-041-3

Printed in Sweden by Studentlitteratur, Lund

ISBN 91-44-23761-8   5   6   7   8   9   10 | 1992 91 90

BIOGRAPHY

Nancy Paul is an American who lives in England and works in the UK and Continental Europe. She is the mother of three growing children. Ms Paul trained as a psychologist at the University of Montana, U.S.A., and works as a management consultant to successful British and International organisations and is Director of Paul Management Associates. She also has a private practice in psychotherapy and is a tutor on the Management Programme of Brunel University where her Interpersonal Effectiveness Seminar was chosen as an outstanding course by The National Training Index. As well as writing a number of books and articles, she is engaged in research concerning the effective use and development of people in organisations.

Ms. Paul enjoys a wide range of hobbies and interests ... music, skiing, mountaineering, swimming, gardening, pets, having fun and enjoying people.

DEDICATION

To those who loved me and helped me...
    My children, D.T.M.C., my friends and family;

To those who taught me so much...
    My clients, my students, my friends...

This is your book to share with others who are searching and growing.

CONTENTS

INTRODUCTION   iii

BEGINNING   v

EFFECTIVENESS QUESTIONNAIRE   vii

CHAPTER 1   1

CHAPTER 2   10
   Influences on How You Behave

CHAPTER 3   24
   Understanding People and Behaviour

CHAPTER 4   49
   Presentation Skills: Verbal and Non-Verbal

CHAPTER 5   78
   Non-Verbal Assertiveness

CHAPTER 6   83
   Verbal Assertion

CHAPTER 7   93
   Non-Verbal Presentation

CHAPTER 8   99
   Protection Skills I

CHAPTER 9   107
   Protection Skills II

CHAPTER 10   121
   Giving Criticism

CHAPTER 11   125
   Feelings

FINISH   142

INTRODUCTION

This is a book about people — you and me. Working with people as I do has given me varied experiences and introduced me to many concepts and ideas about people: how they develop and redevelop and techniques for doing so. To help us do so I have accumulated many of these ideas and approaches to personal development, used them, changed them and added a few new ones. I have watched people learn them, apply them, and grow with delight, happiness and ambition.

Many people will tell you that change isn't easy — *"No pain - no gain "* they'll say. Yes, at times, that's true. On the other hand changing — which is the discovery of you, your resources, power and individuality — is also very exciting and great fun, and can be as easy as it is hard.

This book is about how to make change easy. There are ideas presented to prompt you to think in different ways and exercises to give you practice at dealing with people and situations differently.

So now off you go. Start at the beginning, go at your own pace, and enjoy the trip.

BEGINNING

How would you like to have an adventure? A discovery trip in which you meet the self-satisfaction of rediscovery; particularly rediscovery of knowledge and assets which have been old friends, tried and true. Plus exciting new discoveries and thrilling successes as you journey through new territories? This journey is, as you have guessed, the adventure of *you*; *who* you are; *what* you are and *how* you are.

It's easier than you think to rediscover you. The original you was designed and endowed to be happy, effective and content, so you have the capabilities within yourself to be effective and happy. You were born with them. You either have not learned to use your skills, abilities or talents, or you have learned other things which are not as effective.

The journey is easy if you remember some simple guidelines. There isn't much around that is new, so you may already be familiar with many of the ideas presented here, so much so you might call them common sense ... and it is. In fact, we call this the *Common Sense Approach*.

The *Common Sense Approach* has three rules:
First: *Be You* — Don't try to be a Superman or Superwoman.
Second: *Keep it simple*. Set easy goals and simple actions. Most people give up or fail because they set goals which are too difficult or complicated. But you want to succeed, so keep it simple and make it easy.
Third: There are two parts to you. *You* as an individual, and *you* relating to others. They are equally important, so get them in balance, the I and the We.

To begin, we need to find a starting place. There is a questionnaire on the next page. When you fill this out, you will find out how effective you are in using your personal skills and abilities and how effective you are in dealing with others. When you have finished, look up your score to see where you stand. How effective are you? How much room for improvement is there?

Now make three lists:
1. The *situations* which you don't handle well and would like to improve.
2. The *people* you have difficulty with.
3. *You* — Things you would like to change about you.

Remember the common sense rule: Keep it simple — no more than three items to each list. If you have more, put them all down, and then choose three. Save the others for another time. Your lists are now your *objectives*. The target of how you want to be, and what you want to be able to do at the end of your journey.

Now off we go to find the *Real You.* Remember, "It's common sense", and "Keep it simple".

EFFECTIVENESS
QUESTIONNAIRE

This is not a test. This is a questionnaire which may provide you with some information about your skills with people. There are three answers for each set of questions. Will you read through the questions and tick the answer which comes the closest to what you would actually do, not what you think might be right, but what you would do in each situation. Do it as quickly as possible.

1. You are driving in your car and have stopped at traffic lights. The lights change, but before you can move on, the person behind you is sounding their horn at you. Do you:

_____ 1. Feel embarrassed and flustered.

_____ 2. Acknowledge with a head nod and move on.

_____ 3. Swear, shout or shake your fist.

2. You have an appointment in a part of town which is not a safe place to be. You arrived by taxi and arranged to have a friend meet you. You have been waiting for well over an hour on the street corner in the rain, when your friend finally arrives. Do you:

_____ 1. Unemotionally enquire why they were late.

_____ 2. Angrily tell your friend how you feel about being left.

_____ 3. Get in the car, slam the door and say nothing.

3. You see some kids tampering with your neighbour's car. Do you:

_____ 1. Watch so you can identify them.

_____ 2. Call your neighbour.

_____ 3. Shout, "Stop that".

4. You have been asked to work overtime for the third time this week. You have done so before on the other occasions, and tonight you have an important engagement. Do you:

_____ 1. Say you appreciate their problem, but you won't work.

_____ 2. Say, "OK", but forget and leave at quitting time.

_____ 3. Tell the asker, "Don't be ridiculous".

5. You have a young subordinate or acquaintance who gets frightened easily and seems to be afraid of you. Do you:

_____ 1. Say, "That's ridiculous, I'm a very harmless person. If you play straight with me, I'll play straight with you.

_____ 2. Ignore their fear and get on with the work at hand in a calm and cool manner.

_____ 3. Make a point of a chit-chat with the person in a light or humerous way.

6. You have a colleague or friend who smokes in your home or office, even though you have made it known that you don't like smoking. Do you:

_____ 1. Ask them to please put out their cigarette; that you don't like smoke.

_____ 2. Tell others how unreasonable and inconsiderate they are.

_____ 3. Tell them how inconsiderate they are for smoking when they know you don't like it.

7. You are at dinner with friends when a husband and wife start arguing. Do you:

_____ 1. Try to sort it out.

_____ 2. Tell them to stop acting like children and spoiling everyone's evening.

_____ 3. Ignore them or put music on to cover the noise.

8. You see someone about to do something accidentally which could hurt them. Do you:

_____ 1. Shut your eyes and hope for the best.

_____ 2. Shout, "Stop".

_____ 3. Calmly say, "Be careful".

9. One of your young subordinates or friends is being confronted aggressively by one of your colleagues. The confrontation is loud, but the subordinate seems to be handling it. Do you:

_____ 1. Leave them alone.

_____ 2. Interrupt and tell your colleague he has no business talking to your subordinate like that.

_____ 3. Sit them down and try to reason it out.

10. You have gone for an appointment at an arranged time, and are kept waiting for close to an hour with no information given to you. The person offers no reasons and gives an insufficient apology. Do you:

_____ 1. Say or think, "Stuff this", and leave.

_____ 2. Say, "That's OK".
_____ 3. Say how uncomfortable you are at being kept waiting without being told why.

11. You are heading a committee of people who have been working well together for some time. In general communications are very good, but two of the members are having a disagreement. Do you:
_____ 1. Insist they stop this and be friends.
_____ 2. Leave it to them to sort it out.
_____ 3. Sit the two down and talk it through.

12. The company bully is picking on a shy quiet person in your department. They don't seem to be dealing with it and you are getting very concerned. Do you:
_____ 1. Say in a firm voice, "Stop it".
_____ 2. Ask the person to sit down and talk about it.
_____ 3. Say nothing.

Now turn to the Scoring Sheet and transfer your choices to it.

Scoring sheet

To score your questionnaire, first transfer your answers to the scoring sheet by encircling the numbers you chose as the answers for the twelve questions. For example if you chose the answer to question one as 3, encircle the 3 in column B, question 1, and so on. Having done that, if the number you chose is the same as the number in column X, then circle the number in column X as well.

After you have transferred all of your scores, total *the number of circles* in each of column (A), (B), (C).

Questions	A	B	C	X
1.	2	3	1	2
2.	1	2	3	2
3.	2	3	1	3
4.	1	3	2	1
5.	2	1	3	3
6.	1	3	2	1
7.	1	2	3	3
8.	3	2	1	2
9.	3	2	1	1
10.	3	1	2	3
11.	3	1	2	2
12.	2	1	3	1
Totals				x 5

	Enter in Triangle 1	Enter in Triangle 2	Enter in Triangle 3	Total score Enter on Effectiveness Scale

Put the total for (A) in the triangle space 1; (B) in triangle space 2; (C) in triangle space 3.

Next total the circles in column X multiply by five and enter the total score on the effectiveness quotient.

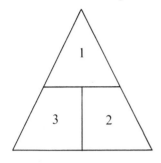

Score

(1)
Assert _____

(2)
Agg _____

(3)
Pass _____

Effectiveness score

0	10	20	30	40	50	60

Effectiveness Scale

Range of effectiveness
50-60 Excellent
40-49 Very good
30-39 Good
20-29 Moderate
10-19 Fair
0-10 Poor

CHAPTER 1

Let's start by having a look at how we manage to deal with people, particularly people who are difficult or who cause us problems. As an American woman, Virginia Satir once said – "It isn't the problem that's the problem, it's coping with the problem, that's the problem."[1] When we talk about "coping" we are actually talking about behaviours. How we behave with people who cause us problems is to use what we call "coping behaviours".

In The Beginning

Looking at coping behaviours, we see that there are two we all use. They are called the "inherent" behaviours. Inherent, because they are both instinctive and learned. They start out as instinctive, but are soon shaped into certain patterns by learning. We know that as small babies we are capable of using these behaviours as a means of staying alive. We communicate our needs to the world by using these behaviours. They are ready for use the minute we are born. However, we know that we change the way we behave as we grow up and learn to fit into our family's system of behaving. We are constantly learning and modifying our behaviour as we grow, so although these behaviours may have started out as instinctive, the learned modifications start from Day 1.

Passive Behaviour I - U+ Inferior ⟵⟶ Aggressive Behaviour I+U- Superior

Figure 1 Behaviour Continuum

Look at the diagram in Fig. 1 and you see the two behaviours we are describing. On one end of the line, or continuum, there is the behaviour described as *Passive Behaviour*, on the other — *Aggressive Behaviour*.

Passive Behaviour
Passive Behaviour is based on an *attitude* we have about ourselves which is basically *Inferior*. It says, generally, "I'm not as good as other people. Perhaps I'm more awkward, not as clever, not as pretty or handsome, or just not as capable. Well maybe there are some things I can do which are as good as, but usually,

1

when I measure myself up, I come out on the bottom." A shorthand way of describing this is to say I — (less than) U, the rest of the world, who are better than I am, or U+ (I—U+).

The *feeling* most commonly experienced here is the feeling of fear. Either pure, raw fear or various forms of it — being afraid, tense, nervous, on edge, flighty. Another feeling commonly experienced in this position is sadness. It is sad, isn't it, when you think about walking around in the world feeling inferior and putting yourself down.

The *behaviours* most commonly engaged in are called "getting away from" or avoidance behaviours; withdrawing, giving up, giving in – "anything for a quiet life", taking the back seat as a supporter, never a leader; and deferring to others' ideas, decisions, opinions, etc.

At the other end of the continuum, have a look at the other people walking around up there. We find that the attitudes are quite the reverse from down there in the passive end. It says, "Well now, there's something I'd really like to tell you. When it comes to looking at me compared to the rest of the schmucks in the world, we know one thing for sure, I am better then you;" so my *attitude* about myself is that I am superior. "I am more capable than you." "I can do things faster, or better and am simply the superior intelligence." "I am better (or I+) than you, the rest of the world who is inferior (or U—), thus I+ U—."

The *feeling* most commonly experienced in this position, is anger. That doesn't necessarily mean great explosive anger, although it can be. There are those other feelings of anger called irritation, annoyance — you know when you, "just get under my skin."

The behaviours that we engage in from the angry position are behaviours of domination. I take, I demand, perhaps I command, sometimes I do more. I humiliate. Patronising is also a behaviour which says "I am better than you." Consider this one too as aggressive: the position of "I'm OK, and you?" "Fascinating, are there other people in the world? — amazing." People who sometimes take this position walk around in the world solely concerned about themselves and totally involved in the 'wonderfulness of me'. Sometimes these are people who live in the Ivory Towers of the academic establishments who are so inward-thinking and sadly involved in their own little world, that they don't see other people. This might be considered one of the most aggressive stances: to discount the existence of other people; to treat them as if they were not there. Another extreme of aggressive behaviour, is sarcasm. It is aggressive and

2

dangerous because it is damaging. It is dangerous because it appears to be innocent fun. You don't see the injuries caused until after the event. Sarcasm is fun on the surface. It is a way to get close to people and break down some discomfort barriers. It's a way of finding pseudo-personal relationships. The reason they are pseudo is because it only looks as if you're getting close, by the give and take and bantering here and there. It does damage because the arrows go in unobserved. You don't see them until later, when you start to hurt and then put your hand up to your chest and find you've four arrows stuck in you and you've lost six pints of blood. Sarcasm does damage outside of immediate awareness and it isn't until later that the damage is discovered. Have a look at sarcasm, be careful with it, and wary of it.

One behaviour
There are some learned people who say that's not actually the way behaviours are. We don't walk around displaying two separate behaviours. They say there is only one behaviour and that is *Passive/Aggressive Behaviour*. To understand this, it helps to go back and talk a little about God, or Mother Nature, or whoever your creator was. Inside every human being, God or Mother Nature instilled a striving to be as healthy and as happy as possible. That's why you have pain mechanisms to tell you "Oh, oh, that hurts — stop", because you might do physical damage to yourself if you don't. Futhermore, you have emotional pain mechanisms which say, "Oh, oh, that hurts. Stop that." These mechanisms are alarm systems which help keep us physically and emotionally healthy.

Passive behaviours are unhealthy for you; unhealthy in this way. Each time you say, "I'll say something next time", or avoid confrontation about an issue which makes you look bad, for instance, it makes your emotional health go down. There comes a time, eventually, when you cannot continue doing this damage to yourself so you have to take a different action. An example is to remember the concept of trading stamps.[2] You may remember that with trading stamps, each time you made a purchase, you also received some trading stamps. You collected these until the book was full, then you could cash them in. Using the same concept, each time your idea is put forward and you aren't given credit for it and you say nothing — each time someone makes a joke out of what you are trying to say; each time someone makes fun of you or humiliates you in public and you still say nothing, a stamp gets put in your book, until your book is full. When the last stamp goes in the last page of your last stamp book, nature's cutoff switch takes over and says, "that's it, that's enough". When that happens you get one free trip up there to aggression and you cash in all your stamps; and aggression

'Another extreme of aggressive behaviour, is sarcasm. Sarcasm is fun on the surface. It does damage because the arrows go in unobserved.'

feels good! Feeling angry causes a hormone to be released in your brain which makes you feel good. It gives you a high. It feels good to get rid of all the pent-up frustrations and irritations.

However, like any drug-induced "high", as the drug wears off, you get withdrawal symptoms. You feel bad. Furthermore, you feel guilty. As you feel guilty, you start the slide back into Passivity. When you feel guilty, you usually remember your Mother talking to you, shaming you for losing your temper — and then you feel worse. "I told you you would turn out just like your Father, (or Mother)." Spurred on by guilt, you make a decision to be in control of your feelings and behaviour, and are determined to "become a nicer person". What you in fact do, is to go to the store room and ask the storekeeper for another stamp book to start a new stamp collection. Because your objective is to, "become a nicer person", you ask for a few extra pages to be added. The bad news is, that, despite all your good resolutions, you will cash them in again, because this is outside your control. It is nature's way of cleansing away your emotional injuries, and nature usually wins.

Bad *v* Inappropriate Behaviour

There is no such thing as "bad behaviours". Aggression, for example, when used appropriately, is effective and necessary. It gets people to do things quickly. When you want short term results, in times of crisis for instance, use your aggressive approach. However, each time you use aggression the other person puts a stamp in their stampbook. This means the next time you deal with that person, it will be harder, because they have been building up their stamp collection. For example, people who scream, shout and bang the tables at meetings, at first get results, but as they continue, others pay less and less attention to them. As they get less results they escalate, and for a time, the new aggression achieves the desired effect, but once again people will stop paying attention to them. If they continue using the aggressive behaviour approach, they'll have a heart attack, burn out, or change their personalities completely. Aggressive behaviour is physiologically damaging. It wears out the body because of the constant "gearing for a fight".

Defensive Aggression

There is also a case to believe that aggression stems from fear, and is used as a defence mechanism. There's an old saying which says "the best form of defence is offence". When people who use this feel afraid or vulnerable they become prickly, sometimes nasty or angry, which puts a barrier around them to keep people away, and it works most of time. They stay untouched. However, they pay the price of loneliness. Difficult people are not very sociable, and who wants them around?

The Good News

Here we are with the two behaviours, each effective if used appropriately in its own time and place, but not very effective as a general operating style. Let's now look at a separate behaviour style, one which is out of the Passive/Aggressive swing which can be used as a general operating style.

If you look at Figure 2 you will see a third behaviour. This is *Assertive Behaviour*. It is different from Aggressive or Passive Behaviours. Different because it is solely learned. You are not born with it. Assertive behaviour is based on the *attitude* of *SAMENESS*. My attitude about myself and about you is that we are more or less the same. "I recognise that there are some things that I can do that you cannot, and there are some things that you can do that I cannot, so we come out fairly level. Also, because I don't know something or because I sometimes fail, it doesn't detract from my self-esteem, or me as a person." This is a major difference between Assertive and the other behaviours.

By saying that I am + and you are +, or I+ U+, it does not mean that we are all

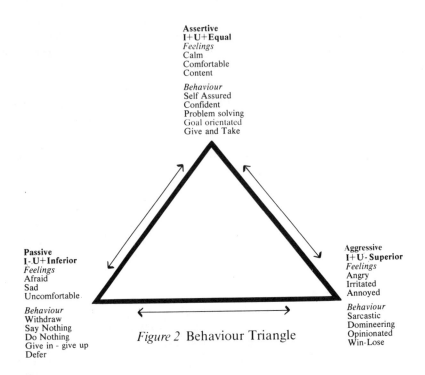

Figure 2 Behaviour Triangle

Assertive
I+U+Equal
Feelings
Calm
Comfortable
Content

Behaviour
Self Assured
Confident
Problem solving
Goal orientated
Give and Take

Passive
I-U+Inferior
Feelings
Afraid
Sad
Uncomfortable

Behaviour
Withdraw
Say Nothing
Do Nothing
Give in - give up
Defer

Aggressive
I+U- Superior
Feelings
Angry
Irritated
Annoyed

Behaviour
Sarcastic
Domineering
Opinionated
Win-Lose

perfect or perfectly wonderful. We are not. It is better, though, to recognise shortcomings and failings in ourselves and others and accept them as part of you being you and me being me, and accept ourselves as not being perfect. We are led to believe that we "can" be perfect and that we "could" know everything. The truth is that we do not have the equipment to be perfect. The human system is an inefficient and imperfect system. For example, you do not "see" others. What you see is not a direct translation of someone, it is an interpretation which your brain does with data that it has picked up. You don't "hear" someone. What you hear is a perception of what your ears pick up. All our data goes through a processing system in the brain, which is an interpretation. We believe we "know the truth", but that, too, is subject to interpretations, and may or may not be fact. On the other hand, if you do wish to be perfect there is a way. It is called the "bio chip"; a micro chip which can be implanted in the brain, and with this you can have almost direct interface with the world. All you have to do is to back your brain off to a computer and you can have access to all of the information it knows instantly. The computer will be able to read your thoughts, so you don't actually have to "do" anything. Just think about it. Marvellous. There is just one little snag. You won't really be a human, you'll be an android.

6

But, you *will* be perfect – all knowing and never making a mistake. If, however, you would prefer to remain a human being, you have to give up the idea that you can be perfect and accept that you have flaws. You have yours and I have mine. We are individuals. We are *different* and *equal* in our differences. My self-esteem is mine and is defined by me. Your self-esteem is yours and defined by you. It is up to each of us to take charge of our self-esteem and definitions of ourselves.

When you give up the idea of pursuing perfection and can accept yourself and other people, flaws and all, you *feel comfortable* and *self-confident*. Another feeling may be one of genuine excitement. A different kind of excitement to the one of the chase and the kill, it's the excitement and pleasure of knowing that you can deal with situations; of knowing that you are in control of you.

Assertive behaviour is thinking behaviour. The result of thinking is that we are more concerned about what is effective, and how to solve problems than winning or getting even, etc. We call this *problem-solving behaviour*. Assertive behaviour means knowing what you want, being able to ask for it in such a way that you probably will get what you want without denigrating your self-esteem or my self-esteem. Aggressive behaviour means taking what you want at the expense of the other person's self-esteem.

There is a continuum between Passive Behaviour and Assertive Behaviour, and also between Assertive Behaviour and Aggressive Behaviour. If you are Passive, then aim for the Aggressive side of Assertive. If you are Aggressive, then practise Passivity, because when faced with real life problems and real life people, we tend to fall back on our usual behaviours. If you are Aggressive and you practise being Assertive, you fall back to Aggressive. What we want to do is to learn a range of behaviours with our fall back and main operating position as Assertive. There is a time to be Passive, when it is best to say nothing, and there is a time to fight, perhaps to fight for your life. Making these decisions of which to do when, comes under the control of Assertive Behaviour, and that is the behavioural style which should be in charge most of the time, with the other behaviours at your disposal when required. Remember, there is no such thing as "bad behaviour". There are times and places for all three. It is knowing when to use which, and how, and with whom that is the key.

EXERCISES

Look once again at the questionnaire on page vii. The behaviour scores will tell you if you are Passive or Aggressive or Assertive.

High scores might mean:

Passive High Score: In general you hold back and don't show your skills and abilities as well as you could. You probably let others take control and have power more than you need to.

Assertive High Score: You tend to act unemotionally and perhaps act or get involved in others' problems when you needn't.

Aggressive High Score: You are too controlling and dominating and could easily frighten people and/or tend to discount the ability of others to act, think or feel.

A well-balanced behaviour triangle would have an even number of scores in all three behavioural modes.

Now look at two of your lists from Chapter One — Difficult Situations and Difficult People.

With each situation, what would be Aggressive Behaviour, Passive Behaviour, Assertive Behaviour?

Which do you use?

Which would be more effective?

Difficult Situations   Behaviours I use

_____   _____
_____   _____
_____   _____
_____   _____
_____   _____
_____   _____
_____   _____

Difficult People	Behaviours I use
_____	_____
_____	_____
_____	_____
_____	_____
_____	_____
_____	_____
_____	_____
_____	_____

Set your goals: How I need to react in a bad situation is:

A._____

_____

B._____

_____

C._____

_____

How I need to deal with these problem people is:

A._____

_____

B._____

_____

C._____

_____

CHAPTER 2
INFLUENCE ON HOW YOU
BEHAVE

As you have seen, we have three behavioural styles, or the potential for three behavioural styles. The explanation of why we choose to use certain ones at certain times can be found in a number of areas. To start the explanatory process, let's take a journey inside and look at the master controlling agent for all behaviours, the brain.

Brain

It all takes place in the brain. Your brain is the centre which stores, selects and controls the operating systems for behaviours. For purposes of illustration, we can say that the brain has two parts which house these behavioural systems. We

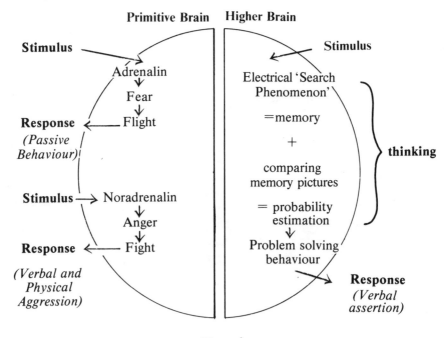

Figure 3
Brain Model

label these the primitive brain and higher brain, although technically we are talking about the hypothalamus and the cerebral cortex.[3] These labels refer to their evolutionary influences. The primitive brain has changed very little since our human development began. In structure and function you would be hard pressed to tell the differences between human and animal. The Higher Brain, the cerebral cortex, is the significant difference between human and animal. This part of the brain has evolved to set us apart from the rest of the animal world, and makes us superior in the animal kingdom. Have a look at Figure 3. You will see the two brain parts represented in diagrammatically. Which part of the brain used at any one time and the specific programming executed, is directly due to family and cultural conditioning, and to a lesser extent, instinctive behaviour.

Feeling Brain

This is the sequence of events which takes place in the Primitive Brain. A stimulus is perceived by one of the sensing organs which sends a message to the brain; e.g., "eyes see sabre tooth tiger hiding behind tree." The message is transmitted speedily to the primitive part of the brain, and a chain of events occurs. Depending on the learning from past experiences, a specific part of the little hypothalamus responds and responds by secreting a hormone which activates the pituitary gland, which produces a hormone which zooms down and activates part of the adrenal gland. This produces the hormone called ADRENALIN. When adrenalin is released into the system it creates the feeling of FEAR. This fear feeling sends messages to the brain to tell the body to get itself running — FAST. Pyschologists call this the FEAR-FLIGHT response.

In a similar sequence of events, the perceiving sensory organs relay messages to the hypothalamus (men with clubs approaching) which, because conditioning activates a different area, sends out different chemical messages, which end up with the secretion of NORADRENALIN which creates the feeling of ANGER. The anger feeling tells the brain to mobilize the body to defend itself and FIGHT. This is called the ANGER-FIGHT response.

Although the process is identical in animals and humans, we have lost the physical capabilities to defend ourselves: no fangs, no claws, can't run very far or very fast because our muscles and bone structure are no longer suitable for fast or distant running. We have humanized the response somewhat, i.e. flight now becomes "mental flight" or in other words, the Passive Behaviours. Most of the fighting we do these days is verbal, so we have substituted Verbal Aggression for fight, although we still engage in a fair amount of the physical kind.

Because the behaviour which is initiated in this part of the brain is based on *feelings*, we call this the "feeling" part of the brain, and these two behaviours "Feeling Behaviours".

Note: The time delay between the stimulus being perceived and the resulting behavioural response is practically nil. It happens as quickly as snapping your fingers.

Thinking Brain

The process in the other part of the brain is somewhat different. Once again the senses perceive a situation or event. This time however, the sensings activate the cerebral cortex which sends an electrical current across its memory files looking for identification of the sensings. When it identifies the stimulus we say it "remembers it". Generally, it finds a number of memories and builds up a composite picture not only of the stimulus but of the associated memories of the past experiences of the stimuli. That is the memory function. When it has retrieved a number of memories it weighs them up not only for identification, but actions and outcomes of the actions. That is called "probability estimation". The two processes combined are called THINKING. The culmination of thinking leads to "Goal-directed behaviour". For example, "eyes see sabre tooth tiger approaching." C.C. (cerebral cortex) stimulated. Remembers, "sabre tooth tiger killed cousin"; conclusion: "can't fight it and win." Remembers, "sabre tooth tigers can outrun man." Conclusion: "can't flee." Remembers: "Sabre tooth tigers can't climb trees." Conclusion: "Would be safe in a tree." Goal-directed behaviour. "Find tree fast and climb it fast!" Of course, our subject was successfull in thinking of this option, otherwise humans would all have been eaten, the Higher Brain would not have evolved, and you would not be here today reading this book.

When we are dealing with humans as the cause of our problems, the resulting goal-directed behaviour is then labelled Assertive Behaviour, since it fills our criteria of Assertive Behaviour. We recognize the situation; remember past experiences, sometimes so quickly that we are not aware of it, weigh up outcomes, and decide which would be the most appropriate. Since the activity of the Higher Brain is thinking, we call it the "Thinking Brain".

Note: The higher brain process is more electrical than chemical. This electrical process takes time, especially when compared to the chemical process of the "Feeling Brain". Therefore, *thinking takes time.* If you want good quality think-ing responses, remember it takes time, so take your time. If you are required to give quick or snap answers, the chances are there won't be much of the Higher Brain involved.

'There is a special relationship between the two parts of the brain (primitive and thinking). They are reciprocally inhibitive.'

Compare the Two

There is a special relationship between the two parts of the brain. They are reciprocally inhibitive. That means they operate in an on-off manner. When one is on the other is off. When you are thinking you are doing little or no feeling. When you are feeling, you are doing little or no thinking. When emotions are high, thinking is low.

One last note. The Primitive Brain is very small – tiny in comparison to the Higher Brain. It's about the size of a pea; hence the term PEA-BRAINED. How often we use that tiny Pea Brain instead of utilizing the resource it took millions of years to develop and think. Remember the common sense phrase, "engage brain before opening mouth", instead of giving a "pea-brained" response.

EXERCISE

Think about the times you have "panicked" and did things which you regretted later, or the times you lashed out in anger, or ran away or "shut down" — i.e. became very quiet, said nothing or did nothing. Now list them in the "situations" column. In the next column put down your Pea-Brained response (PBR) and next to it your Thinking Brain Response.

Do write these down. You will be amazed at how much your brain will remember when you encounter a similar situation in the future.

Situations	PBR	TBR

Cultural Models

Since there are a number of behavioural patterns to choose from, how is it we learn to do the particular things we do? There are a number of explanations. One of the most influential reasons being the culture or society you were born and raised in; the strongest variable being whether you were born a boy or a girl, for there are very definite characteristics and behaviours which are encouraged and discouraged for each. When you consider this, don't confuse cultural dictates with what you may believe is right or what was encouraged in your house. That may be different from the cultural mode of how boys should behave and how girls should behave. In general, and note we make generalizations, there will be exceptions to the rule, we still believe men and women should behave as follows:

The OK Cultural Norm   *The Not OK Cultural Norm*
AGGRESSIVE MEN   PASSIVE WOMEN   PASSIVE MEN   AGGRESSIVE WOMEN

The model of the strong, silent, macho male is still considered the "OK role" for Western Man. The complement to that role is still, in the majority, the passive little woman, who is seen as soft, caring, warm and dependent. Non-passive women are viewed as aggressive, strident, domineering and very Not-OK. Little girls are still encouraged by the media and educational systems, and the culture in general, to consider ambition and brains as not-OK, relying instead on looks and warmth to attract a male protector and provider. Although womens' lib has been with us for over twenty years, only slight indentations have been made in these role expectations for women.

Men who do not fit the bill, who find the rough, tough life unacceptable, prefering intellect to contact sports, are perhaps quiet, sensitive and show feelings, are often labelled weak and wets, particularly by some Macho Women.

There is plenty of incentive for these role types to change, some particularly for men. It is this macho scripting, which encourages men not to show feelings, to be brave and strong, and that allows men to punish their bodies to the point that they die on average 8 to 10 years before most women do.[4] It is role expectation which causes stress and stress disease. With this much at stake, why does this role persist? The problem is deeper and more difficult for men than women, for if a man were to choose the Passive Role Model he pays a price which is far greater than the price women pay. He has his sexuality questioned and is suspected of being homosexual. It seems to be far more threatening for a man to have his masculinity questioned, than for a woman's femininity to be in doubt— although this too is not easy for women. It would appear that men have more of their personal identity tied to their sexuality than women do. To question this then, may be perceived as a threat to existence. So here we are caught between a rock and a hard place. Staying with the traditional roles can cause unhappiness, limited freedom, stress, and in some cases, early death. On the other hand changing roles invites comments on "changing sex" or in some cases, open opposition and violence, as with the case of backlash in the Women's Movement. What is wanted is the best of both worlds for both. The best of the masculine and the best of the feminine is sometimes called androgyny.[4] Androgyny[2] is different from Unisex because women will still have the feminine charms and feelings while being able to think, be decisive and can be action-oriented. Men have the strengths of masculine scripting, finding excitement in achievement and performing, while being able to care, be close, have fun, and live longer at the same time. What is needed is the personal equipment to put this into action, and a guide for a fairer system of roles and behaviours for both men and women. However, back to the present, the behavioural systems we have available from our culture favour aggressive systems for men, passive systems for women. To utilize a more flexible approach, we need new behavioural systems, which allow the use of all our capabilities.

EXERCISES

In the culture I was raised in, *men* were expected to be:

_____

_____

_____

In the culture I was raised in, *women* were expected to be:

_____

_____

_____

In the culture I was raised in, *men* were considered not-OK if they were:

_____

_____

_____

Women were considered to be not-OK if they were:

_____

_____

_____

In the culture I live in today, expectations of how *men* should behave have/have not changed because:

_____

_____

In the culture I live in today, the expectations for *women* have/have not changed because:

_____

_____

One reason it is difficult for *men* to change their cultural scripting is:

_____

_____

_____

One reason it is difficult for *women* to change their cultural scripting is:

_____

_____

_____

Two things that *men* could do to make their lives less stressful and more fulfilling are:

_____

and

_____

Two things that *women* could do to make their lives less passive and more fulfilling are:

_____

and

_____

Family Models

An even stronger influence on how we learn to behave is our families: mothers and fathers, brothers and sisters. Each family has preferences about *how* people do things, i.e. behaviour. It makes sense when you consider it. If there were not a

'Family Models'

general pattern for behaviour you would not have a sense of belonging to your family. It would be difficult for others in your family to recognize what people mean and what they are doing if each person behaved differently. It would be difficult to organize the activities of a family if they did not do things in the same way. For example, how could you enjoy a good time together if one person's idea of *fun* was going for a walk, another's five-aside football; another's playing Scrabble; and yet another's listening to a Brahms symphony? It would be even harder to have a family argument if one person's idea of *arguing* was to run to their room and hide; another's to change the subject; another's to get something to eat; and yet another's to yell and shout. To have an interaction with others in your family, you learned that there are preferred ways of doing things. Your original learning is to imitate your parents' preferred style of doing things. You learned by imitation. Children simply copy what they see their parents doing. It is the easiest and most efficient learning system in existence. You can remember, I'm sure, seeing children dressing up in Mum's or Dad's clothes, pretending to be grown up. You do that "pretending" all through your childhood, gradually putting it in operation for yourself. Some families adopt an Aggressive mode for dealing with people and coping with problems, some a Passive style. There are those who "hog" the decision making, say "no" to everything, and never take "no" for an answer. Sarcasm is perhaps the modus operandum for having family fun. For them, the best form of defence is attack. Compromise is known as "heads I win, tails you lose". The Passive family doesn't like raised voices, can't say no, and when it comes to decisions the favourite saying is, "Oh, I don't know, what do you think?" Victimology is often a favourite game in this family, blaming circumstances and everyone else in the world for their plight, i.e., the Government, the Labour Party, the Bosses, the Schools, the people next door, etc., compromise is "anything for a quiet life". Then there are some who have an Assertive approach to life. Give and take is the family philosophy, or, "All for one and one for all". Although it operates as a unit, each individual is important, and is treated with respect, regardless of age. Yes is used as often as No, and when No is used it is accompanied by reason and explanation. Compromise is known as "Sometimes I win and sometimes You win". People who come from this type of background are successful people. It is by looking at these people, studying what they learned and how they effectively dealt with people, that gives us the Common Sense Approach which we can now teach to others who may not have effective coping behaviours easily at their disposal.

Have a look at your models: your Mother, your Father, brothers and sisters. Boys usually model after their fathers, girls after their mothers. Sometimes, our models acted inappropriately and we decided not to be like them. If our Father or Mother was particularly violent or painfully passive, we may have modelled after the other parent. If both were inadequate we would have had to look further, perhaps outside the family, an uncle, aunt, teacher, the person next door. If we could not simply absorb our role model which is the natural way, but had to pick and choose from others, we find that we lose a bit of spontaneity. Incorporating fuller systems which we could use more freely would be an objective to aim for here.

Your Models

As a guide to reclaiming some of the parts of you that you learned not to use along the way, have a look at your family's operating systems. Identify those which are effective and those which are ineffective. Where did they come from, your Mother, your Father? Who are you more like, your Mother, your Father? Which systems do they use today? Are they effective?

Now set yourself some goals. Write down three things you would like to change about you in the way you deal with people and cope with problems. These are your goals for this programme. Learning the skills necessary starts on the next page. Working through the exercises at the end of this chapter may help you arrive at these goals.

EXERCISE

Our family's favourite behaviours were Aggressive, Passive, Assertive (which):

_____

Their favourite slogan was, "*Anything for a quiet life,*" "*Live and let live,*" "*Don't let anyone step on you.*" Or, no family slogan or other slogan:

_____

_____

Anger
When it came to anger, my *Mother* would show that she was angry by:

_____

_____

My *Father* would show that he was angry by:

_____

_____

When I am angry today, I show it by:

_____

_____

which is like my Father/Mother.
I'd like to be able to be more/less openly angry.

_____

Someone who shows anger appropriately is:

_____

Sad
When my *Father* was sad, he showed it by:

_____

When my *Mother* was sad, she showed it by:

_____

Today, if I feel sad, I show it by:

_____

which is like my Mother/Father.

_____

I'd like to be able to feel sad more/less:

_____

Someone who shows sadness appropriately is:

_____

They show they are sad by:

_____

_____

Happy
When my *Father* was happy, he showed it by:

_____

When my *Mother* was happy, she showed it by:

_____

Today, if I feel happy, I show it by:

_____

which is like my Mother/Father.

_____

I'd like to able to feel happy (more/less).

_____

Someone who shows happiness appropriately is:

_____

They do so by:

_____

Say No
My Father could/could not say No to my Mother.
My Father could/could not say No to the children.
I was/was not allowed to say No back.
Sometimes I could say No back if I paid a price; (was reasonable) (devious) (persistent) (risked being punished) (feel guilty).

My Mother could/could not say No to my Father.
My Mother could/could not say No to the children.

Sometimes I could say No back if I paid a price; (was reasonable) (devious) (persistent) (risked being punished) (feel guilty).

Today, I can/cannot say No at work.
Today I can/cannot say No at home.

I can say No if I pay a price which is:

_____

Two people I would like to say No to are:

_____

Someone who says NO in an OK way is:

_____

Decisions

<Answer yes or no>

My Father made the decisions in our house _____

My Mother made the decisions in our house _____

No-one took decisions _____

Today

I take decisions at work _____

I take decisions at home _____

I take decisions without hesitation or worry _____

Two situations where I would like to be more decisive are:

_____

_____

Someone who makes decisions easily is:

_____

Compromise

In my family, compromise consisted of:

Mother/Father winning _____

Mother/Father giving and taking/not giving in _____

Today I compromise by:

_____

Situations I could come to compromise on are:

_____

_____

Family Attitudes

Our Family thought they were in general better than others _____, inferior to others _____, about the same as others _____.

I believe I am superior/inferior/about the same as, most people.

My family was: A critical family _____

A sarcastic family _____

A hypocritical family _____

A self-righteous family _____

A worried family _____

A happy family _____

Do-gooders _____

Today my family is (which of the above) _____
I would like us to be a _____ family
A family I admire is _____
they _____
_____

Two things which I learned from my family that I would like to change are:
_____
_____

Two things I did not learn from my family that I would like to learn are:
_____
_____

CHAPTER 3
UNDERSTANDING PEOPLE
AND BEHAVIOUR

Now that you know how your behaviours work, let's move on to the next step which is to begin to learn new ways of dealing with people.

To do this, a model called the PAC Model is helpful.

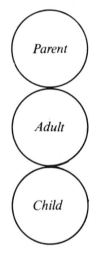

Figure 4
PAC Model

The PAC Model is based on a personality theory called Transactional Analysis.[2] It says, basically, that every human being has a personality which has three parts in common. These three parts are based upon some universal truths.

Universal truth number one, is that we all were children. We all started in the same way; were brought into this world in the same way and went through the same development processes. The developmental processes and the behaviours associated with them, are stored in that part of the personality we label the *Child*, (see Figure 4).

Universal truth number two, is, all people have parents. Not necessarily your biological parents, but parents in some shape or form; adults of the human species who showed you how to behave and took care of you. This is true otherwise you wouldn't be here right now, as in Western culture a child cannot survive until it is eight years old without that kind of caring and direction.

Universal truth number three, says that as humans, we all have a cerebral cortex, otherwise we could not be called human. If there is an impairment to the cerebral cortex, then such people are usually regarded as subnormal. The cerebral cortex is in charge of thinking—rational, linear thinking, and it is our conscious contact with the outside world.

In the TA Model, these are called "Ego-States". An ego-state is an integrated system of feelings, thoughts, and attitudes directly related to unique, observable behaviour. Each ego state system has its own set of observable behaviour uniquely its own. If we take those three parts, we say that, for labelling purposes, the activities related to each can be thought of as our parenting, our thinking and our childhood development.

By observing behaviour (gestures, mannersims, etc.), listening to words, speech patterns and delivery, it is possible to tell which ego system you or the other person is using. A useful way of explaining the PAC System is to go through the process of development. This way you will see how ego states are used and developed which will help you understand them and give a better insight into what we sometimes call "problem" people.

The Child

Overleaf is a picture of your personality when brought into the world, (see Figure 5). As you can see, the personality of the Child is just as a baby appears, a little bundle attached to a parent, totally dependent on that parent for care, protection and love.

Although the structure for your personality is there, it has not developed the neurological or physiological structures necessary to be able to use it. This part of the child we have when we are born, is called the "Free Child", or the "Natural Child". The Free Child has one task to begin with, and that is to survive, and to survive in the best possible way. Located in the Free Child is the survival equipment. The Free Child communicates with the outside world, making its needs known in order to survive. Here are the very basic needs and wants. How we

25

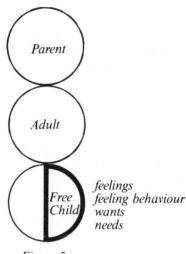

feelings
feeling behaviour
wants
needs

Figure 5
Free or Natural Child

communicate them is through the "feeling behaviours", passive and aggressive. When a baby is hungry or uncomfortable, it cries. When a baby is lonely or frightened, it cries. If unresponded to, baby demonstrates rage, which is very angry aggressive behaviour. When the baby is happy and content, it sleeps, gurgles or coos. This is how baby gets its' needs met, expressing them through the feeling behaviours. They are spontaneous and immediate — and they expect immediate attention. They want things done NOW. It is almost as if something is written in the brain of baby which says, "You are the prince or princess of the world, you are the only one that has any importance."

The Adapted Child

Babies however, soon discover that parents have needs and wants which need looking after. There now starts a competition. Anyone who has had a baby in the house will know what it is like to be kept awake night after night with baby needing to be fed at awkward hours, or crying, interrupting a peaceful relaxation. It is this kind of "needs competition" that finally makes the parents begin the push for baby to learn something different. They say,"Wait a minute, you are not the only person in this world, there are these big people here too, and we have needs." We all have our little Child inside of us, at all ages, which wants to eat; that wants to sleep; that wants to have fun, with time to himself and time to relax. The pressure on the baby to learn and to change happens quite early, for example, learning to sleep through the night; eat at more sociable hours etc. That becomes *the* developmental issue between 6-18 months; learning to adapt, to be sociable and fit in with others. The behaviours we express in this manner, becoming aware of the needs and wishes of others, we call Adapting, and part of the personality which is in charge of this is called the "Adapted Child". (see Figure 6)

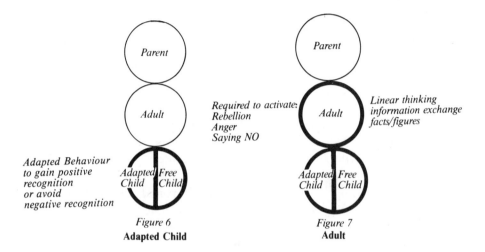

Figure 6
Adapted Child

Figure 7
Adult

The Adapted Child will say, "OK, wait a second now, I've got to do something different. I want to make you smile and make you love me." The incentive to do this is quite simple. It's the basic need to survive. Buried inside every child is the uncertain feeling of death unless they are taken care of. So children "know" the importance of keeping Mother and Father around. They also know how good it feels to have their approval. What is learned is to adapt to please Mum and Dad. Later the behaviour generalizes to others. Women learn to do the stereotypical things like being nice, quiet, etc., and assume an expected Passive behaviour role. Men learn to be achievers, doers, performers. Practising these socialized skills keeps the child busy until around 18 months to 2 years when the second ego state — The Adult, is brought on-stream.

The Adult

The programming of this ego has been taking place since birth, but does not become noticeably functional until this age. (see Figure 7)

27

Programming this ego state, and learning to use the conscious, cognitive function, leads to the most noticeable and dramatic stages of development. Perhaps you can recall little two-year-olds you have known, and know that there is good reason to call this the "Terrible Twos", for the ignition of this ego state seems to be fairly fraught and stormy, especially for the parents. The issues are two: Learning to think and using your thinking to solve some of your problems and to take care of yourself. This leads to less dependency on the parents and therefore self-identity emerges.

As you will recall, the Adult is the seat of rational linear thinking. That makes it possible for a child to think, analyse and estimate probability. But here's the rub. At this age the favourite word is "No". "Do you want to sit down?" "No!" "Do you want to stand up?" "No!" "Do you want to watch television?" "No!" "Do you want a drink?" "No! No! No!" and subsequently throwing a temper tantrum. This is the issue: becoming an independent person with your own identity. NO is the word, ANGER is the feeling, REBELLION is the behaviour. It is important that a child goes through this negative stage, because it seems to be necessary[5] to excite cerebral cortex activity and to be able to think fully and demonstrate those thoughts. Perhaps why the little child is so angry and rebellious is that it is probably afraid of letting go. It wants to hold on desperately because it still feels the need to be strongly attached to the parent and reacts in self-defence with anger. In a way it is the cutting of the umbilical cord. "You are trying to push me out into the world", "You are trying to make me think", "You are trying to make me solve problems, and if I solve the big problems like potty training, that means that you, Mother, will be free, and I'm afraid that you might not stay around to take care of me." Ambivalence is the order of the day, clinging at one time and angrily rebellious at another. They hold on so that you don't go too far away, but push away at the same time to sample independence. In order to make this push against parents, to become free, and a separate person with his or her own identity, anger and rebellion must take place.

This is important for some of you, because you may remember a time when NO was not allowed; not an acceptable word for you to use in your house. If so, you may have some trouble today, since being rebellious is an important natural phenomenon. Maybe some of you still have some two-year-old rebelling to do. Another phenomenon sometimes happens here and that is people getting stuck in rebellion, where fault is found in their own ideas or opinions, and being critical or negative is the family mode. Now they are known as "negative people". Their first word is "NO". They criticise rather than get actively involved and usually look for the other side of the argument. Here some learning is required to express ideas and decisions instead of staying on the sidelines, criticising and sniping.

28

At last we get to be three years old, and start to come out of the stormy rebelliousness. The child has learned, become more independent and capable of doing things. They can dress themselves, get out of bed, open the door—which is sometimes at six o'clock in the morning—to have a run down the road in their pyjamas. They start investigating the world a bit more, and continue programming their Adult, spending most of their time between three and six years old asking questions. They want to know everything. Show me, show me, show me, the big word being "Why?" As they become more capable and assured that the parents are not going to leave them, the rebelliousness subsides and the child becomes more social and grown-up.

The Parent

The next ego state, the Parent, comes on line in the UK at about five, in America at about six, in Scandinavia at seven. This is the age when children can go to school. They are now capable of leaving mother and father, because now, inside their heads, in transistorised form, mum and dad are there telling them what to do; what not to do; how to think, behave and feel. They are up there, mother and father, programmed into their heads, just as if someone slotted in a microchip with them etched on it. Actually, it is quite good because it is, as we have

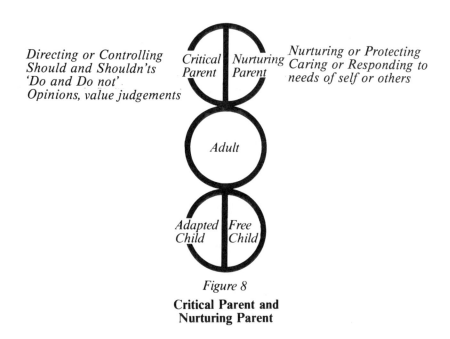

Figure 8

**Critical Parent and
Nurturing Parent**

29

seen, the easiest form of learning, to "ingest" your parents. Now you have your Parent ego state to tell you just as you had your parents; how to behave, what to do, and what not to do. It is sometimes called the morals and manners department, full of the "politics", the "shoulds"and "shouldn'ts", "the dos" and "don'ts".

The part described here is more accurately called the Critical Parent, or Controlling Parent, because by giving you directions on how to behave, it controls and limits your behaviour. It seldom encourages or urges you on. From there, you express opinions and make value judgements. The importance of this ego state is two-fold. It provides you with an easily learned, spontaneously-expressed, guide line on how to live and behave. However, because it is from the past, it may be out-of-date, or inappropriate to situations you find yourself in today.

Another part of the Parent is called the Nurturing Parent. It tells you how to take care of yourself and responds to the need of your Free Child. For example, if you feel a bit cold and you think "I'd better shut that window", that is the Nurturing Parent responding to the needs (feeling uncomfortable) of the Free Child. If you are hungry, your Nurturing Parent tells you to stop what you are doing and get food; if you are uncomfortable in your chair, your Nurturing Parent suggests getting up and stretching or walking. If you are with a person who makes you feel uncomfortable, your Nurturing Parent tells you to stay away from that person, or conversely, if you like someone, Nurturing Parent says "go ahead, be close".

Your Critical Parent, "talks" to your Adapted Child. Unlike the Nurturing Parent, rather than respond to it, it motivates the Adapted Child to behave in a certain way, telling it what to do, and how to do it, and criticizing it when it performs badly. If you have made a stupid manoeuvre in the car, your Critical Parent would say in your head, "What did you do that for?" Your Adapted Child says, "I shouldn't have done that, that was stupid." That is your Parent telling your Child to modify its' behaviour.

Secondly, you use your parent system on other people. You respond to others needs, or Free Child, from your Nurturing Parent, or your Critical Parent tells their Adapted Child what to do and what not to do, and criticizes them when it thinks they are not behaving in a way it wants them to.

To continue with our saga of development, the Parent ego state comes on stream, as said, between 5-7 years old, and is developed and exercised until around 9-10 years old. The child now has the full complement of personality equipment and "could" survive on its own. But there is more to be done in our Western culture to get the child up to adulthood standards and prepare it for life, so parents are still required to be in charge of them and care, as further development takes place. Around 8-10 years, the whole process starts again, laying down the next layer of personality.

The Next Layer of Personality

The Child ego state goes through further development when the child usually re-experiences dependency. Children at that age suddenly become "clinging", wanting to be next to Mum as she peels the potatoes, sit on Dad's lap as he watches T.V., and once more wanting the light left on at night, and to be put to bed. Little boys who were once the indomitable explorers of the world, are now no longer willing to walk to Cub Scouts on their own. Thumb-sucking, bed-wetting, and a reluctance to perform, or even go to school, might occur as the child cements, or re-cements, the bonds between itself and the parents, making sure it can safely experience dependency thus ensuring the ability of forming dependent bonds with others when it is older.

The cementing of ties also seems to ready the child for the next big push for autonomy and independent identity. Learning to think for yourself, becoming independent and in charge of your decisions and priorities. It's the two-year-old stage second time around, called here "adolescence". The issues are the same: becoming a person separate from your parents with your own personal identity. Adolescents seem to disagree with most everything their parents say or stand for, particularly their value systems, but at the same time, still needing an amount of caring and reassurance. The typical teenager says, "I don't know why I even have to live in this house." "This is the most repressive house I have ever seen." "I would much rather live in Joan's house down the road." "Her parents at least understand her and let her do things." "It's like a prison camp around here — Mum, Mum when did you say dinner would be ready, and I can't find my socks." Sometimes it's quite a shock to parents, particularly if the child didn't rebel much at two and combines the twos and teens rebellion into one. We all do this, the push, push, push but hold onto me.

The work on developing our independence and thinking continues until, around 16 to 18, we start on the second programming of the Parent. This is when older teens become insufferably intellectual or overbearing about virtually

31

everything — fighting for all the causes. They act more sophisticated and grown-up than grown-ups in certain areas, and every generation of young adults believe they are the first intelligent thinkers to be born, and discover all the idealistic causes their elders have out grown. They use and express—over express their parents would say — the power and range of their Parent Ego State. Fortunately, having exercised this muscle, they then begin to recognize their parents and others as intelligent, caring human beings again.

The second stage development is usually completed by 21, at which time there is a final break in the parent-dependent relationship, when they leave home and establish an independent existence, as capable adults, deciding, expressing and being responsible for themselves and their lives.

Until fairly recently we thought that was the end of the story. Development of personality was thought to be like physical development, that we stopped, fully developed, around 21 when we reached adulthood. But the theory did not fit the evidence. As Erik Erickson[6] noted, people continue to change and develop and do so in various depths, all their lives, and do so in what appears to be seven-year cycles.

We recycle our personality, adding new layers, or trying to fill the gaps of previous layers, every seven years; establishing dependency relationships with marriage or special relationships, further rebelling against Parent values as we establish our own ways of life and discover new ways and establish our own morals and values. Parent further develops as we ourselves become real parents and enter into child raising.

During the seven-year recycles, we seem to pay more attention to some development stages than others. A major push against established value systems for women takes place around 32—when women start looking around for other meanings to their lives. Women who married and have been raising children, usually return to work, or seek a career, sometimes in antithesis to marriage in order to seek personal identity. Divorce is common, the median age of divorce for women being 32. Women who have chosen work and career also start to look for other meaning in their lives, and either marry or start families at this age, going against the interests and activities of their 20's.

Men also experience a phase of searching: looking for answers to life, the universe and everything. At 42, now commonly called mid-life crisis, men see the down-hill side of their life; can see the end of their lives, sometimes for the first time. Men who were company men, leave the company to set off in new directions; men who were conventional family men, often leave a marriage to go to live on a houseboat with the 19 year-old-blonde and exchange their business suit for jeans and sandals. Many previously rebellious men become "respectable". For example, the leader of one of the first radical revolutionary groups in the United States changed his life style at this age, and is a multi-millionaire with a seat on the stock exchange at Madison.[9]

We continue to change, grow, change directions and emphasis in our lives until we die — and perhaps even after that event. Some of these issues will occur and re-occur, such as the rebellious one, giving notice that there is work to be done here. Your personality is not set. You are constantly developing and changing.

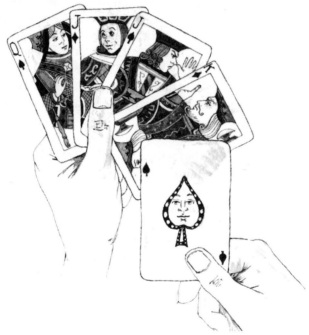

'The PAC model is based on a personality theory called Transactional Analysis. For clarity the personality is divided into parts, the Nurturing Parent, the Free Child, the Adapted Child, the Critical Parent and the Adult.'

Changes to Reclaim Power

As times change and the world changes, so do each of us change. Looking at new ways of dealing with people is then a natural part of the change cycle. When you become more effective, you will be more in charge of your life, and more in charge of the changing cycles of your life.

One area to change is the Adapted Child. Too often we have been programmed to over-adapt, to be too concerned about what others think of us rather than expressing our views and ideas. Shrinking the AC (Adapted Child) a little, *but not completely*, would be an appropriate exercise for some of us. Looking at our values, finding out about what YOU think, what YOU want, and reclaiming some of this area for YOU as an individual and not dependent for your self-esteem on what others think of you. Also since the majority of our Parent ego state was programmed when we were children, some of that programming does not serve us well in these times. Because of radical changes in our culture — mobility, technology, etc., what your parents did and knew, may have little application for you in your work or life style. Clear some space up there for some new ideas and guide lines on how to run your life, how to deal with people, which suit the current times. It isn't as if we don't have the potential to use all our ego states, we do. It is simply through learning that we have gradually put our energies into certain areas, withdrawing it from others. The personality is a closed system similar to a hydraulic system. That means, in order to enlarge the Adult, for instance, one or both of the other ego states, has to shrink. The energy is there. We need to redistribute it, our target being an evenly proportioned ego state system.

Another useful change would be for those of us who are afraid of the word "NO" to learn to use it. "No" is a defining concept. It tells others where they stand, and also allows you to programme and plan your life. You can keep to schedules, take on realistic amounts of work, stay away from people who take advantage of you, by saying "No". There is also power in anger. Being angry is a natural phenomenon, we all do it. It is protective, and sometimes may be the only way to get someone to respond to you. There is a time and place to be angry. If you have been taught that it is dangerous or impolite, you have lost a most valuable piece of behaviour.

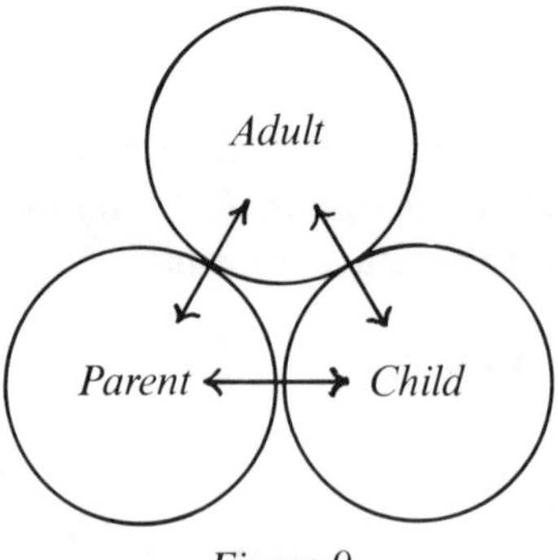

Figure 9
**Direct Contact
between Ego States**

Other areas to firm up are the boundaries between the Parent and Adult and Child and Adult. You don't really walk around in the world with your Parent, Adult and Child, stacked up one on top of each other. They are arranged more like the picture in Figure 9.

As you can see, each ego state is touching the other, and can interact directly with each other. Just as you competed with your Parent for control of your thoughts and decision making processes when you were a child, so your Parent still competes with your Child for influence of the Adult. When the Child interferes with this process, we call it contamination from feelings and past experiences. You have experienced this, for example, seeing someone who reminds you of a person from the past who you didn't like, and having this colour your approach to this person. This is shown in Figure 10.

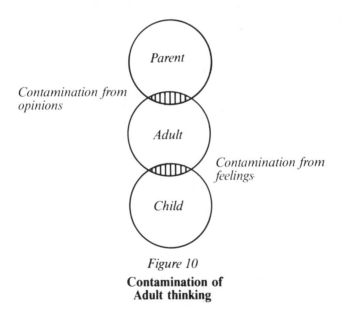

Figure 10
**Contamination of
Adult thinking**

We sometimes react suspiciously, overact, or hear criticism where none is intended. Our target here would be to step aside from these "feelings" and see people and situations as they really are, and respond appropriately to these people as they are in the here and now.

The second source of contamination is the Parent's encroachment on the Adult. It slips in, taking over the reasoning process, inserting its' experiences and value judgements in place of fact. This is probably the most common form of contamination, and all of us do it at one time or another. However, it is this process which gets us into trouble with others more than anything else. We get into arguments and conflicts, which often end in shouting matches because we act as if our value judgements are facts and therefore "the truth". You can usually tell when this process is in full swing because the volume increases as the exchange of "I'm right", — "No, you're not", "Yes I am", gets underway. This is sometimes called "Uproar" — because the roar goes up. Here are some examples of opinions masquerading as facts.

"That chair is badly designed".

"A person in your position should know better".

"A little knowledge is a dangerous thing".

They are Parent contaminations because the statement is delivered as "the truth" or fact, rather than prefaced by "I think" or, "In my opinion". Pulling the Parent back, recognizing that opinions and value judgements are important, but knowing they are those and not Adult fact, would keep personal relationships less fraught and problem solving less heated and more effective.

You may be wondering if we use our ego states equally, and if all ego states are similar in size and content. The answer is no. It depends upon how you were raised. Some people are constantly Adult; they show no opinion; they show no emotion or anger. They are facts and figures people like computers. Their conversation is only about facts and figures. We would say that their Adult is huge and that their Parent and Child ego states have shrunk. Some people have an oversized Critical Parent. They assume a superior role, telling people what to do and what not to do, and criticize frequently. These are the people who sit on the outside of a group, snipe and make comments, but do not join in. They reveal neither their Child nor their Adult, which is risky, but find fault with others, or find the flaw in every process or "the reasons why it won't work".

Then there are others who have a large Nurturing Parent, take care of or "mother" everyone or everything but discount their own needs. Others with an over-large Child, play around, are rebellious or disruptive. They find it difficult to give a straight answer and usually find something humorous in every transaction. To make room for their over-large Child, they have a small Parent and a small Adult ego state.

It isn't as if we don't have the potential to use all our ego states, we do. It is simply through learning that we have gradually put our energies into certain areas, withdrawing it from others. The personality is a closed system similar to a hydraulic system. That means, in order to enlarge the Adult, for instance, one of the other ego states, or both, have to shrink. The energy is there; we need to redistribute it, our target being a fairly evenly proportioned ego state system.

Putting it into Practice

What do you do with them now that you've got them? Let's now put these concepts to work for us. We all have a Parent, an Adult and a Child ego state. I have, you have, we all have. The way we communicate with each other is between these ego states. My Adult can communicate with your Adult. My Child can communicate with your Child. My Parent with your Parent, my Child can communicate with your Child. My Parent can talk with your Child, my Child with your Parent etc. *A unit of communications between ego states is called a transaction.* Looking at these, and understanding them, is called Transactional Analysis, or T.A. for short.[8] We can have a very good idea about what is going on between people just by watching them, listening to the tone of voice, the words, watching gestures and mannerisms. This gives us important information about which ego state is used, the "intent" or motivation of the people involved, and a good guess at the outcome. In fact, this is so precise, that there are laws which govern these communications. There are three of them. Learning to use and recognise them gives more control and effect in our communication processes.

Laws of Communication

It isn't just the words that we use, but the *value* of the words that we use that is important (see Figure 11). For example, when our Adults talk to each other, it is an exchange of information, facts, statements of reality ("that is", or "there is" statements, etc.) For example, if I asked you what time it is, it is my Adult asking your Adult for information, and the information comes back from your Adult, which is the time in this case. This gives us a complementary transaction, A to A (see Figure 12). If my Parent talks to your Parent, we usually exchange opinions and value judgements, or concerns about *something else* or *someone else*. Parents play a lovely game called "ain't it awful?"—usually about the younger generation. How many times have you heard. "Isn't the younger generation terrible?" and "When I was a lad down t'pit", or, "These new micro-computers are going to put all these people out of work, don't you think it's terrible?"

The Child ego state exchanges feelings, wants, likes, dislikes. For example — "Would you like to go out after work and walk along the river?" "Yes, that would be super, I'd enjoy that."

The Parent to Child transaction is confirmation of, or an attempt to establish

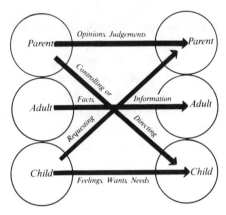

Figure 11
Transactions

roles: Top dog and Bottom dog, Superior and Inferior. The Parent says: "I'm in charge here". "I know best". "I know what is good for you". "I am superior", or in other words, I+ U—. The Child responds by saying, "OK, you do know best", or, "I am not as clever as you", *complying* with the definition of I— U+. Or it *rebels*, saying "No, I won't" "You can't make me", or "Why should I?" If, for instance, you have ever said to anyone, "Look at me when I'm talking", you may remember that the answer might be, "OK", with a furtive glance, thus complying to your superior role, or, "No, why should I", then arguing, thus rebelling against the Superior Role, yet staying in the "*One down position*".

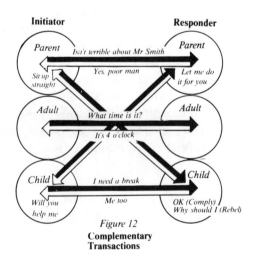

Figure 12
Complementary
Transactions

Communication Law 1. When the ego state which was targeted, receives the transaction, and returns it to the sending ego state, there is a parallel or *complementary transaction* (see Figure 12), and because we all understand the nature of these transactions, understand the value of each, we have communications which can go on indefinitely.

Using this rule is one of the most important aspects of being effective. Express yourself clearly and firmly from Adult so people understand you, resisting the temptation to play games, argue or get upset, or get angry, critical or sarcastic, when involved in problem solving or trying to make yourself understood.

Communication Law Two, says sometimes, however, the ego state aimed at does not respond, but a different one does — and not back to the original ego state, but to a different one. When that happens, we say we have a *Crossed Transaction.* When this happens, communication ceases. For example, if I said to you, "What time is it?", a possible crossed transaction might be, "You should remember your watch in future", or that, "You should be able to tell the time", — that is a cross-up from the Parent to the Child. The Child can also respond to the Parent, thus crossing the transaction. For example, "Don't ask me", "Tea time", or "Why are you always picking on me?" The critical point of crossed transactions is that we no longer have the understood communication link. We are now talking at crossed purposes. The communication process stops, or goes badly, or the arena changes. This is described in Figure 13.

'Sometimes we operate on more than one level at the same time.'

One transaction which we usually don't like and is often damaging, is the Critical Parent to Adapted Child transaction. It is called *criticism*. It says, "I am the

39

big person and you are the little person". "I can define who you are and what you are". "I can make myself feel OK by making you feel Not-OK". If you adapt, and respond by saying OK, or if you rebel and say "so what", or argue, we have a parallel transaction, and according to the laws of communication, we will continue on the one up and one down level indefinitely.

We now know we can alter this by applying Rule Two. Cross it up from our Adult by saying, "OK, you and I can talk, but it will be about facts", or from Nurturing Parent. Sometimes you may recognise that criticism is a defence against being vulnerable or hurt. If so, we may have success by taking care of this hurt

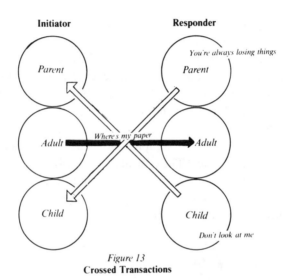

Figure 13
Crossed Transactions

Child from an understanding or nurturing position (Nurturing Parent). This is called understanding or empathy. We reassure the Child and then offer problem solving from the Adult. Turn off the feelings, so you can turn on the thinking.

Two-Level-Transactions

Sometimes we operate on more than one level at the same time (see Figure 14).

It may look as if we are having an Adult to Adult conversation, but you can tell the other person is holding back either criticism or annoyance, or upset or hurt feelings. When this happens you are transacting on two levels at the same time, the fact level and the feeling level. *Communication Law Three says, if you are transacting on two levels, the fact level and the feeling level, the feeling level will determine the outcome of the relationship.* If so, it makes sense to find out what the feelings are or what the criticism is about. If there is fact and feeling mixed, the feeling will influence the outcome more than the facts. For example it might look something like this. You are annoyed because a subordinate is becoming arrogant and is stepping on your toes, but you don't say so. Instead you say, "I was wondering about that report you gave me yesterday, did you read it thoroughly before you gave it me?" The answer might be, "Yes, I read it." "Did you read it from cover to cover?" "Yes." "Very interesting, you actually read the whole thing?" Now, if the answer continues to be "yes" and the person ignores what else is hinted at, he

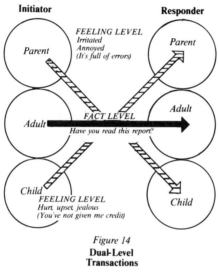

Figure 14
Dual-Level
Transactions

might be labelled as "over-ambitious for his capabilities", or, "not open to criticism". Perhaps a person is hurt or upset by past remarks or events, but does not bring it into the open. Imagine a secretary speaking to her boss. "Here are the papers you asked me for", and drops the papers on the desk and quickly turns away, with a hurt look on her face, sniffing back tears. If the boss ignores the feelings being demonstrated, she will be deemed to be insensitive, domineering and gossip will be put about concerning, "bitchy, insensitive women managers".

Tell — Not Show

It is apparent there is something wrong, but they can't tell or don't want to tell you what it is they're upset about or displeased with. The trick here is to be able to get people to *tell* you what they are annoyed or angry at, or hurt and upset about, *not show* you. Ask for information A to A, while showing we recognise their discomfort, criticism, upset etc, A to P or A to C, thus taking the heat and feeling out of the situation and finding out the facts about the problem, and prompting them to use Adult to report on feelings or criticisms to pursue problem solving. Some ideas of how to put this into practice are contained in the "Dealing with Criticism" section.

Here then, are some ideas of areas to reclaim the talents and capabilities you've not used or had forgotten about, to make you a more effective You.

EXERCISES

PAC-MAN

Adult: Adult expresses statements of fact/reality/probability estimation.

Three statements from Adults are:
(Example: That chair next to the door is brown.)
1. _____
2. _____
3. _____

Parent: Critical Parent expresses judgements/opinion/criticism, and uses directive statements (you should, do's and don'ts, etc.)

Three statements from Critical Parent are:
(Example: That chair is too old-fashioned for this room.)
1. _____
2. _____
3. _____

Nurturing Parent: Nurturing Parent expresses and responds to needs and wants, gives care, and expresses care and concern.

Three statements from Nurturing Parent are:
(Example: "Eat if you are hungry, sleep if you are tired.")
1. _____
2. _____
3. _____

Child: Free Child expressess wants/likes, body needs, physical and emotional feelings.

Write three:
I like: _____
_____
_____

I don't like: _____

_____

_____

I want: _____

_____

_____

I don't want: _____

_____

_____

I feel: _____

_____

_____

I don't feel: _____

_____

_____

Adapted Child: Expresses behaviour based on directives from parents (or internal Critical Parent)

My Mother always wanted me to be _____
and _____.
My Father always wanted me to be _____
and _____.
My Mother wanted me to grow up to be _____
_____.
My Father wanted me to grow up to be _____
_____.

Choose which of the following that decribes you:
Today I am (not concerned, very concerned, moderately concerned) about what people think of me.
I (always/sometimes/seldom) try to get things right.
I (always/sometimes/seldom) try to please others.
I (always/sometimes/seldom) try to hide my feelings.

Look at the above and choose one of the following:
_____ I am more concerned about what others want me to think, say or do than I am myself.

43

_____ I am more concerned about what I want to do, say or think than I am about others.

_____ I am equally concerned about what others think of me and what I think of myself.

Two things I would like to change to suit me rather than others are:

_____

and _____

PAC Transactions

1. Complementary
A to A, Exchange. Adult to Adult are exchanges of facts or information.
Give three examples of an A to A exchange.

1. _____

2. _____

3. _____

P to P, and Return. Parent to Parent exchanges opinions, judgements, or competes with others for the Parent (Top Dog) position.
Give three examples of a P to P exchange.

1. _____

2. _____

3. _____

C to C, Exchange. Child to Child is an exchange of feelings, likes, dislikes.
Give three examples of a C to C exchange.

1. _____

2. _____

3. _____

P to C, Exchange. Parent to Child exchanges are about roles. Who is in charge? Who is superior, who's the subordinate?

1. _____

2. _____

3. _____

C to P, Exchange. Child to Parent exchanges are about roles. Who is the subordinate; who doesn't have to think or can't do?
Give three examples of Child to Parent exchanges.

1. _____

2. _____

3. _____

Crossed Transactions

Type One Crossed Transaction
A to A with a P to C return (facts crossed by opinion or putdowns).
Give three examples of a Parent-Crossed Transaction.

1. _____

2. _____

3. _____

Type two Crossed Transaction
A to A with C to P return (facts crossed by can't do, can't think, disruption, change of subject, play).

1. _____

2. _____

3. _____

To cross P to C from A to A, see Chapter on Dealing with Criticism.

Two-Level-Transactions

Top Level
A to A, Transaction about facts, information etc.

Feeling Level
C to P Upset or hurt, grievances.
(Example: I don't think you and I had better work together.)
Give three examples.
1. Top level _____

Feeling level _____

2. Top level _____

Feeling level _____

3. Top level _____

Feeling level _____

A to A, information or indirect criticism.
P to C, hints of annoyance, disapproval or criticism.
(Example: Have you read this report *thoroughly?*)
Give two examples.
1. Top level _____

2. Parent level _____

To elicit information about the Parent annoyance or the Child feelings, without the person acting out from these States, see the Chapter on Dealing with Criticism.

PAC Stages

Left home at _____ age.
Finished college/university at _____ age.
First job at _____ age.
Second job at _____ age.
Married at _____ age.
First child at _____ age.
Last child at _____ age.
Career change at _____ age.
Divorced at _____ age.
Remarried at _____ age.
Became religious at _____ age.
First child in school at _____ age.
First child left home at _____ age.
Last child left home at _____ age.
Death of first parent at _____ age. (your age)
Death of second parent at _____ age. (your age)
Retired at _____ age.
Questioned the purpose of life for the first time at _____ age.
Changed life style at _____ age.
Concerned about death at _____ age.

CRISES:

1. _____

2. _____

3. _____

Life changes

Is there a pattern to your life's phenomena? _____
Are there crises? _____
Is there a pattern to these crises? _____
If so, when will there be another? _____
What will it be? _____
What is changing in your life? _____
How is it changing? _____
How have others coped with changes in their lives? _____

What have they done to cope? _____
_____

List three things to do to control the changes in your life.
1. _____
2. _____
3. _____

What changes would you like to make in your life style before it changes you?
_____
_____

CHAPTER 4
PRESENTATION SKILLS:
VERBAL AND
NON-VERBAL

Making a Request

To begin with let's look at you, in control, taking the lead, expressing your point of view, getting people to listen to you and take you seriously, as well as keeping your priorities intact. Structuring your work and activities so that you do the amount of work or activities you are best at, by saying no when you need to.

"Sounds good", you might be saying, "but if it really were that easy, why don't most people do it?" "Why haven't I done it?" That's a good point. Most of us get enthusiastic about ideas, make resolutions to put them into practice, make attempts and fail. The reason is we either make it too complicated or don't have a clear idea of how to do things differently — or both. Here, then, is a guide for you to follow. It shows you what to say and how; what to do and how. It is simple and brief — there are only three steps and that's the key to success — keep it as simple and as easy as possible. Off we go, with our 1-2-3 steps to being effective.

Step 1. *Listen and show the other person you hear and understand.*
Step 2. *State what you think or what you feel.*
Step 3. *State what you want or what actions you want taken.*

Step 1

Listen and show the other person that you hear and understand them.

You may well express surprise that the first step to being a more effective you is listening; and yes, if you are expressing your point of view you are quite right, you will probably not begin by listening. To begin with the listening step is to emphasize it's importance in the communication process. Miscommunication starts by being a poor listener.

These are the things we do as poor listeners:
- we think of what we're going to say rather than listening.
- we jump to conclusions without hearing the other person out.
- we listen to dialogue inside our heads instead of listening to the other person.
- we day-dream or shut off.
No wonder we fail to communicate.

Good listening demonstrates reasonableness and the I+ U+ position. Speaking figuratively, it clears space so the other person can come forward and present their views. It says, "It's OK. I'm neither going to attack you nor will I run from you — you and I can converse on the same equal level."

How to Listen
Being in physical proximity to a person may be enough to hear them. But you do need more. You need to demonstrate that not only do you hear the person but you understand what they are saying to you. To do that, use your eyes and your mouth.

'How to listen. You need to demonstrate that not only do you hear the person but you understand what they are saying to you. To do that use your eyes and your mouth.'

Using your Eyes to Hear

One of the easiest ways to demonstrate that you are listening to a person is to look at them. Looking away demonstrates lack of interest, or fear, or criticism. Can you remember trying to tell someone something that was important to you and they spent their time looking out of the window, or at the floor, or doodling on a piece of paper? One of the reasons for this is explained by the study of neurolinguistics [9]. Neurolinguists say that we use our three senses, visual (eyes), auditory (ears), and kinesthetic (touch/feelings) to take in our information about the world. Of these three senses the majority of us rely on our visual senses, i.e., what we see for most of our information. It could well be that visual people, as well as depending on facial expressions and gestures for information, read lips—either consciously or subconsciously. If you look away while you are talking you are depriving them of a rich source of hearing, and if you look away while you are listening, they believe you are not listening to them.

Looking at the person actually makes your ears hear better by lessening distractions from the outside or day-dreaming. Neurolinguistics has demonstrated that if your eyes are in a straightforward level position your external vision and external hearing are "on" more fully, and that helps you concentrate. Looking at the person, resting your gaze somewhere on their face, will give you that good hearing turn-on.

Your Mouth in Hearing

Listening is a two-way process. It isn't just you absorbing words like a sponge. Just as in using your eyes, you need to demonstrate what you hear. You use your mouth. The talker needs two pieces of information from you: (1) that you are listening and, (2) that you have understood what they say. The first we can demonstrate by looking and nodding our head "yes" or shaking it "no". The second requires more. Because we don't have a direct in-take system from the external world, we all do some kind of interpretation and to put what we hear into a form we can understand and handle. The talker needs to know if the form and meaning of their words which you hear are approximately the same, having gone through our interpretation system, as they were when they left their mouth. The way to demonstrate this is to say what you've heard and how you've interpreted it. This is called "reflective listening". Say some of the words, or the meaning you've put on them, so they can check if you have the "gist" of what they've said. It's like being able to check on a screen or print-out that what you've intended to feed into a computer really has been programmed in the way you intended. Don't, by the way, say "I understand you", or "I hear what you're saying". That's about the most worthless piece of jargon that was ever invented. Tell them *what* you've heard and *what* you think they mean, either by repeating some of the

51

words you've heard, or paraphrasing what you've heard — putting it into your own words.

Another way to demonstrate your understanding is to give back how you feel or what you think about what they've said. Share a similar experience you've had. In other words, match the content from your own experience. That strengthens the communication link between you, and demonstrates fully that you hear and understand.

Here then are the listening steps:
1. Look at the person.
2. Reflect back the words or the meaning.
3. Add your own experiences or express how you feel or think about the subject, or ask questions to clarify or show interest.

One final reason to be more *active* in your listening, i.e., saying something. There is an old psychological law which says: *Passivity escalates aggression in other people.*[10] If you want people to become angry with you, say nothing and don't look at them when they are talking to you. If you are a Passive person and find that people seem to get quite annoyed with you — even though you say nothing, that could well be the reason — saying nothing/doing nothing. It is your passivity that sends them into a rage. So be *active* say something in return. If you are afraid, or don't know what to say, say something, even if it's, "I don't know how to answer you", or, "I have to have some time to think about what you've said".

EXERCISES

Step One: Listening Practice

Hearing
Non-involved: Non-people
Practise listening to people, first in a non-involved way, so that you can practise your hearing. Listen to a discussion on the radio or TV for 5 to 15 minutes. At the end of that time, write down what you remember. You might be disappointed by how little you recall. However, you will find that if you repeat the exercises two more times you may well double the amount you remember.

Non-involved: People
The next step is to listen to conversation between people: Travelling on public

transport is a good place to do this, or in a meeting where you are not involved.
Listen to what is said, then take some time for recall.
Who said what? _____

_____

What feelings were expressed? _____

_____

Who controlled the conversation? _____

_____

What was the outcome? _____

_____

_____

_____

Responsive Listening
Now practise listening and responding. Points to remember:
Look at the person.
Nod your head "yes", or shake your head "no".
Use monosyllabic responses occasionally; such as, "yes", "OK", "right", "no", etc.
Support the conversation by:
> *Reflecting* the words or meaning that the other person uses.
> *Asking questions* to clarify or extend the conversation.
> *Making comments* or revealing your feelings, thoughts, or experiences to build up the support bridge of understanding.

Remember: Use your *eyes* to look at the person. That shows you are listening.
Use your *mouth* to show what you understand.

Do not: Jump to conclusions, hear the whole lot out.
Do not: Respond to what you think is implied or might be implied.
Do not: Mind read — listen!
Do not: Stop listening in order to formulate your response.
Respond *after* you have heard what the other has said.
If you need time, pause, or say you are thinking.

Practice: one to one
Practise with a friend. Have a conversation with a friend. Talk for one minute.

Stage one: Practise looking at the person and nodding your head "yes"or shake your head "No".

Use short comments:

Yes	No
Really	How awful
Fantastic	Terrible
Super	Too bad
Terrific	Dreadful

Stage Three: Look at the person. Nod your head "yes", or shake your head "no".
Say some of the words they have used.
Ask questions about the subject they are talking about.
Make comments about the subject.
Share your knowledge or experiences on the subject.

Listening in Meetings or Groups

If you are in a group of people such as a meeting and are finding it difficult to keep track of who is saying what, write it down, thus:-
Example:

Name   **Points made**

Miss X _____

_____

Mr T _____

_____

Ms H _____

_____

Mr W _____

_____

Secondly,we sometimes find that we have a hard time listening if we have a point to make. Keeping our points in our minds and listening at the same time is difficult. Usually, it is the listening which suffers. Again, write it down, so you can let go of the task of remembering, and listen until you can interrupt or have an opportunity to have your say.

Ideas or Points to say

Example:

Subject: _____

_____

Points: _____

_____

_____

_____

Subject: _____

_____

Points: _____

_____

_____

_____

Subject: _____

_____

Points: _____

_____

_____

_____

Step Two

State what you think or how you feel

Now it's your turn. You've begun by clearing the space for the other person to put their case; demonstrated that you are interested in them; assured them that you will neither attack not run. It's now time to put your side. Your objectives here are threefold: to be clear, informative and direct. Don't beat about the bush Come out with it. Sometimes in our attempts to "cushion the blow" — or what *you* might think is a blow — we succeed in scaring the other person into believing that things are worse than they are. On the other hand, because you are direct it doesn't give you a licence to be rude or aggressive. There is a fine line to walk. The trick is being open, direct and nice at the same time.

Blocks to Directness

Some of the blocks to directness are prohibitions from the past. Sometimes you behave in ways which are not particularly relevant or appropriate to you, but were necessary or more appropriate for your parents or grandparents. There are two variables which influence us in this way. One of these is the "Polite System". The other is adaptations which were made along the way to cover up problem areas or to keep knowledge within the family circle.

The cover-up system is often the result of class mobility, or more accurately, a striving for class mobility. It was particularly acute in the struggle to leave the working class and reach the hallowed ranks of the middle class. It was often

TABLE I

Everyone's Rights and Responsibilities

I have the right to:
1. PRIVILEGE   Set and hold my own values and priorities.
   RESPONSIBILITY As long as it does me no harm nor you no harm.

2. PRIVILEGE   To be treated with respect.
   RESPONSIBILITY To treat others with respect.

3. PRIVILEGE   To be listened to and taken seriously.
   RESPONSIBILITY To talk in a clear way and listen to others.

4. PRIVILEGE   To express my own feelings and beliefs.
   RESPONSIBILITY To be responsible for the consequences.

5. PRIVILEGE   Ask for what I want.
   RESPONSIBILITY To allow others to do so.

6. PRIVILEGE   To say 'no' without paying for it with guilt or other
                    deeds.
   RESPONSIBILITY To say 'yes' when I mean 'yes' and 'no' when I mean
                    'no'.

7. PRIVILEGE   To get all information from superiors or professionals
                    which pertains to me.
   RESPONSIBILITY To ask for that information.

8. PRIVILEGE   Make mistakes which are part of the learning
                    process.
   RESPONSIBILITY To learn from my mistakes.

9. PRIVILEGE   To be the judge of my own worth, time or expertise
   RESPONSIBILITY To use information I have received from people I
                    value.

10. PRIVILEGE   Choose to act passively, assertively, or aggressively
                    as the situation required it
    RESPONSIBILITY To be responsible for the consequences.

necessary to adopt a posture to convince others (and yourself) that you had made it, and any vestiges from the working class were hidden or denied. Often Dad was banished to the kitchen when visitors came round for tea since he insisted that, "A man's home is his castle", and enjoyed sitting around in shirt sleeves and braces, and embarassingly enjoyed brown sauce on everything, much to the chagrin of the socially-conscious members of the family. To make sure these social class deviant behaviours did not leak out, warnings and threats were given to children to "Keep themselves to themselves"; "Keep it in the family"; "Don't wash your dirty laundry in public"; "Keep it private"; "That's family business". Important messages to stop children who tell all from spilling the beans. Unfortunately, these messages are often handed on as part of our operating systems, even though the immediate cause is no longer relevant. Here is an example of how outmoded messages influence the performance of adults today.

A man was recently stopped at an airport and asked by a market research person if he would take part in a survey she was conducting about cars. He sailed through the part about the make and model, revealed that it was a company car and not his own, and could answer how satisfied or dissatisfied he was with the product. But when he asked how old the car was, he replied, "That is none of your business!", and walked away leaving a rather astonished researcher. When he later recalled this incident he remembered something that was an issue in his house when he was a child. "My Father had just moved into a supervisory job and we moved house to a new neighbourhood which was quite a jump from the old one." "There, there was one important factor as to how important you were in the neighbourhood, and that was your car, but most particularly how old it was." "We were cautioned time and time again not to talk about how old Dad's car was, because it was the oldest in the road, and I guess that just stuck with me." "Rather silly when I think about it, especially since now it isn't even my car!" And he has passed this operating message on to his children whom he recalled cautioning in a similar manner. As you will remember from the PAC model, we call these "Parent Messages". They are handed on one generation to the next, even though sometimes the reasons for those beliefs or those behaviours are long past or lost along the way.

Another block to directness is the social system which says "Politeness is being indirect". For example, not asking for what you want because that is selfish. Not talking about yourself, because that is rude and big-headed. Some of the little sayings which carry these messages are: "I want never gets". "Don't talk about yourself, you'll get a swelled head". "Others first". Probably the best message of all is, "Those who don't ask don't want. Those who do ask don't get". That is a rather damnable position to be in. It's called a double bind; damned if you do and damned if you don't. Another message, "Do unto others" is often translated into what has become the Golden Rule of Neurosis: "Do for others what you really want done for yourself"[4]. This is *not* to say to be impolite and don't care about others. Far from it. What we have discovered is that we have to be polite in a different way. The old system of politeness was appropriate for a small world in which everyone shared the same values and acknowledged the same social and human rules. It worked when one generation followed another; grandparents knowing grandparents, parents knowing each other; children learning how to be a grownup from their elders; what kind of work and how to perform was learned by simply following their parents' example. In this fast moving, fast changing world, these indirect systems don't work too well because not everyone shares the same value systems nor operates under the same code of conduct. A new system is required which allows a person to be direct and open without being aggressive.

Everyone's Rights

To help you accomplish this, look at Table I, a guide to help you judge what behaviour or attitude is appropriate, both for you and for other people. These are not legislated rights so don't rush around insisting, "these are my rights and people better respect them." These are messages to encourage you to think more positively about yourself and your capabilities if you tend to be a Passive person. If you are Aggressive, to give you some guide lines about seeing the other person's point of view, putting yourself in their shoes. Notice it says Everyone's Rights. This means I have these rights and you have these rights. I am OK and you are OK (I+ U+). We are equal.

Let's have a look at these. The first one says, "I have the right to *set and hold my own values and priorities*." This means your basic value systems, or priorities relating to them. It also means being an individual; that each of us has our likes and dislikes, perhaps sometimes our own little peculiarities which are important to us but not to others. Because we like one thing and not another, and we are different from one another, it does not give us or anyone else the license to manipulate. We value ourselves and we judge ourselves. So little comments like, "How could you possibly like that!", no longer affect us. However, it does carry a responsibility with it; *that you do no one harm, yourself or anyone else*. This means *real* damage, either physical or real emotional damage. Real emotional damage is humiliating or belittling another person. Hurting their feelings is not real damage.

2. *To be treated with respect.* Many people have a belief that you must earn

respect. This is somewhat different. What is meant is our basic equality as human beings. We all have the right to be treated with the same respect, at least initially. Then it is up to us to act in a responsible manner so people will respect us. Also, if we do not respect others, we should not expect them to respect us.

3. *To be listened to and taken seriously,* is very similar to Number Two. It says first, you have the right to be listened to, but secondly, you have a responsibility to express yourself as clearly as possible and to offer the same right to others: *Be a Good Listener.* However, if people do not listen to you, you have the right to stop talking; ask them to listen and ask them to take you seriously. If they don't, you have the right to not talk with them if you wish.

4. *To express my own feelings and beliefs and be responsible for the consequences.* This is two-fold. (a) To be able to say how you feel, give your opinions, state the facts as you see them. Well, why not? You are a big person now. You are equal to others. That means that your views, ideas and feelings are as important as any-one elses. However, remember that others may not like it, be offended, upset, etc. There are those who say, "Well, so what!" "if you feel the way you do, that's your responsibility". That is very much the licence for the "Me-ism" society where all I think of is me. Think about this. If you do step on someone's toes they have the right to yell, "Ouch, that hurts". Some of us don't care. We have the respon-sibility to care more, to be more aware of the feelings of others. Some of us care too much. We need to remember that you are as important as others, sometimes more so. We tend to look on the dark side; that our actions will provoke others to be critical or angry or upset or hurt. True, others may have these reactions, or they may not. Weigh it up. Even if the response were to be negative, you can deal with it.

5. *To ask for what I want.* The operative work is *ask*—not demand or hope for. Ask allows the other person the same options. It does not pin them down or fence them into a corner with no room to manoeuvre. The objective is to be clear. Let people know what you want. Sometimes you do not get what you want or people do not act as if you are important to them because you do not tell them what you are thinking or tell them what you want. You "hope" that they will be good mind readers, and "nice" enough to give you what you want. Hoping usually leads to disappointment and frustration. Do everyone a favour by talk-ing out loud and asking for what you want.

6. *To say "No" without paying for it either by feeling guilty or doing something to make up for it,* seems to be the most difficult area for people. We have been

trained from the time we were small to be agreeable, cooperative, and "do as we're told". We are taught the two-rule system — "Do as I say, not as I do". That says the big people can say "no" to the little people, but if the little people are not allowed to say no back, and if you were to venture the "no", you did so at the risk of a clout around the ear hole, or someone being very upset and hurt — and you feel guilty, terribly guilty. Others of us found that we could risk a "no" if we were "reasonable", with reasonableness being defined by someone else. We learned to justify, intellectualise, or disguise our priorities, because in a straight competition our wants usually were not judged "reasonable" or important. That, however, is a fallacy, as we saw in Right 3. Also, think about "No" in this manner, that it is simply a refusal to a request for a behavioural act. Nothing more, nothing less. Nothing about you as a person or me as a person.

7. *To get information from professionals & superiors which pertains to me.* Like the above, this has implications for work as well as your private life. As grownup people you are both responsible for and in charge of your life. It is up to you to make the decisions which affect your life. You have the right to get information from people in order to make these decisions. It is part of the responsibility of growing up, becoming an adult. At work when you are charged with the execution of a task or a responsibility, you have a right to all information and facts which you need to learn to do the job and to execute the job to the best of your ability. There are people who hold on to information, or are reluctant in other ways to give you the equipment to succeed in your job. Jealousy, fear, greed, lack of future, these are common reasons. However, you not only have the right, you have the responsibility to get what you need in order to do the job to the best of your ability.

8. *The right to make mistakes* addresses the natural learning process. Trying new things assumes some kind of trial and error behaviour. You can't know it all or do it all perfectly the first time: all the time. Sometimes we are coerced by the idea — ours or others — that making a mistake is the worst possible act a person can do, because it means you are imperfect or deficient in some way. In this kind of coercive system, people learn to deny, cover up and play blaming games rather than admit and take responsibility for their errors.

Mistakes are part of the natural learning process, so think of them in this fashion. A mistake is a problem which needs correction. Find out how to correct it, put it right and move on. Don't spend time blaming, justifying or denying. Accept responsibility for it and put it right.

9. *To be the judge of my own worth.* Think about this. When I buy something

there is an implicit contract of equality; an equal exchange of money for goods or service, nothing about you or them as people. The same is true about work. Your contract of employment is an equal exchange for time, labour, skills, expertise, in exchange for money, working conditions, recognition, reward and job satisfaction. If you are not getting an equal exchange, re-negotiate the contract. What people often do instead is "re-negotiate unofficially" — come in late, take long lunch hours and breaks, skive, leave early, take time off. What employers do is criticize, write memos, keep notes in secret files marked "personal" where they document all misdeeds to justify future actions and spread rumours. How much better for both sides to re-negotiate the contract back to a workable level of equality.

10. *Choose to use other behaviours if the situation calls for it.* Assertive behaviour is best regarded as an effective operating system, from which you can move into other behaviours, Passive or Aggressive as situations demand. There are times to be Aggressive, to fight for what you believe is right, and/or to protect yourself. It is an effective and useful behaviour to have. There is also a time to be Passive, to keep a low profile, to do nothing, say nothing if it does not go against your basic value system. There is also a time to run. All behaviours are good behaviours. Knowing when to do what, and doing so appropriately makes you an effective person.

EXERCISES

Applying your Rights
Think of situations where you needed to think more positively about yourself, and apply your Rights and Permissions.

Taken Seriously
1. A situation where I was put down or not listened to was:

    _____

    _____

    _____

    What I did or said was: _____

    _____

    What I will do/say in future is: _____

    _____

2. An incident where my values or beliefs were questioned or made fun of was:

_____

_____

What I did or said was: _____

What I can do in future is: _____

_____

3. The last time I showed how I felt and was made fun of was:

_____

_____

What I did and said was: _____

What I can do in the future is: _____

_____

4. I was treated with disrespect and/or humiliated when:

_____

_____

What I did was: _____

What I can do in future is: _____

_____

5. When I say "NO" I usually feel: _____

To encourage myself to say "NO" I will tell myself: _____

When I say "NO", most people: _____

One person I find it difficult to say "NO" to is: _____

What they usually ask me to do is: _____

Next time I am asked to do: _____
_____ I will say "NO".

Next time I am asked to lend: _____
_____ I will say "NO".
A phrase I can say to myself to encourage myself to say "NO"
is: _____
_____

6. The people I need information from in order to do my work more efficien-
    tly are: _____
    _____

    The people I need information from in order to make my personal life
    richer/easier are: _____
    _____

    The people who are difficult to get information from are: _____
    _____

    Next time I need information from _____
    I will ask in a straightforward way, and not be put off by any sarcasm or
    put downs they use. I will remember that I am as good as they are.

7. These are the things I find it difficult to ask for: _____
    _____
    _____

    These are the people I find it difficult to ask for things: _____
    _____

    Next time I have to ask (name of person) _____ for
    _____ I will say _____
    and remember I have the right to ask for what I want.

8. When I make a mistake I usually: _____
    _____

    When others make mistakes, I usually: _____
    _____

    Next time I make a mistake:
    I will say to myself: _____
    _____

    I will say outloud: _____
    _____

    If I continue to make the same mistakes, I will: _____
    _____
    _____

9.   Situations where I need to be Assertive are: _____

     Situations where I need to be Passive are: _____

     Situations where I need to be Aggressive are: _____

Clear and Direct

Use some of your new permissions to express yourself, your thoughts and feelings. Here's a tip on how to do that: Use the pronoun "I" — first person singular. "I", when you are talking about *your* thoughts, opinions, attitudes. If you avoid some of the words you have been taught to use instead, you will make yourself very clearly understood. For example, words like *one, you, we* or *it*, in place of "I" have several implications. They can mean me; they can mean you, or they can refer to a principle or social rule, "One does not say such things", what does that refer to? — I shouldn't? You shouldn't? Everyone shouldn't? It is very unclear. There is some confusion here, however, which is the belief that if you say "I" all the time you are being big-headed, self-centred and egotistical. Yes that certainly is correct. However, there is a difference between talking about yourself *all the time* and using the pronoun "I" when you are expressing *your* thoughts, ideas and feelings, and it is only the latter we are advocating. Talking about yourself all of the time *is* aggressive and selfish, and does not lead to two-way communication.

EXERCISES

Who am I?

Step 2: Talking about myself, my thoughts, feelings, opinions.

Finish the following statements with as many words as possible which describe you.

I am _____

I am not _____

I like _____

I don't like _____

I think _____

I don't think _____

When I am sad I _____

When I am angry I _____

When I am happy I _____

The Ring of Confidence

Sometimes we have a difficulty when we are talking about ourselves, knowing how much to say, to whom and when. How many times have you missed a golden opportunity to get to know someone who is interesting, or could be of some help, but didn't because you held back. On the other hand, how many times have you regretted saying too much to the wrong person; paying the penalty of having it used against you at some later time? I think this is a common occurrence most of us have had the misfortune to experience from time to

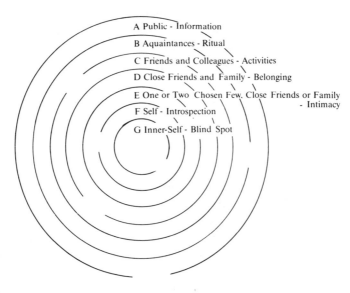

Figure 15 **Information Maze**

time. Have a look at the Information Ring, on page 65. This is a handy guide for getting around such awkward or embarassing moments, and guarantees to cut down on "after-burn" — you know, after the situations when you say, "Why didn't I say such and such", or "Oh, you fool why did you have to say that".

This bull's eye, as some people call it, represents all your thoughts, feelings, behaviours, attitudes and beliefs; in other words, everything about yourself. These rings can be regarded as "information rings". Starting at the centre, where the most private information about you is stored, your inner-most thoughts and feelings, to the outside, where this information carries no risk and is freely given. The outer ring, the A Ring, is the *public ring*. The quality of exchange here is Adult to Adult, involving only information exchange. If you were asked directions, you could easily tell a person, even though a total stranger, with little or no risk to yourself. If asked by a taxi driver what address you wished to be taken to you could tell him, knowing there was no reflection on you personally. A problem has arisen today, however, when people conducting surveys wish to know your opinions or attitudes, e.g., opinion polls, marketing surveys. This is now a riskier proposition since it is revealing Parent attitudes and values and Child likes or dislikes. It can be treated like Adult information if there is *no* connection to you personally, i.e., your name, address, who you work for.

The next level is in the B level and labelled *Acquaintances*. These are people you may recognize either by face or by their name, but know little more about. Perhaps they are people who work in the same office building as you; ride the same train as you every day; or parents of children who go to the same school your children attend. You recognize them, but know very little about them. The kind of communication pattern here is called RITUAL. "Hello", "Nice day today," "Hasn't the weather been terrible, or lovely, or wet, or cold." Weather is a usual form of ritual. The transactions are mainly Adult to Adult, or Parent to Parent. Once again there is very little risk to you as a person.

Moving into *Level C* we are now communicating with people we know better: *friends and colleagues*. Sometimes people are surprised to see these two categories put together, particularly when organizations foster the idea that the work site is for work, and no other kinds of communications and relationships should take place at work. There are two things wrong with this philosophy. Doesn't it seem a bit ridiculous that the people you spend the majority of your waking time with should not be considered more like friends than strangers? Secondly, one of the most important factors influencing the efficient and effective functioning of an organization is good work relationships which operate largely on the informal communications process. But be careful here. There is a difference between friends, friendly discussions and telling all. What we are talking about is telling *more* about yourself; how you spend your time, what you do outside of work, what your hobbies and interests are in order to give a "common ground" basis on which to relate to each other and communicate. This is the establishment of the "Informal Communication System". When the informal system is established, the work environment has less stress and the formal communication system is more effective. Remember we are stressing balance here — not going overboard to the point that more socializing than work is done. The ego states involved here are the Parent, as you express your opinions and judgements and declare your value systems, and the Child which adds to the quality of the communications as you relate on your likes, dislikes, preferences, etc.

Such communications usually are organized around ACTIVITIES, such as work, projects, reports, hobbies. sports and interests. Since more of the content of the Child and Parent are involved, there is now an increasing risk to the person, often expressed by competitions about who is right and who is wrong; who is the best and who is the worst, and what is best and what is worst.

Level D is called the *belonging level* since it involves close personal relationships with either family or close friends, more Child to Child transactions. Since you are now with people you trust, you are able to let your hair down and have some fun together. These are people with whom you can *tell* how you feel, and as you move deeper into the ring, *show* how you feel. The Parent is now involved since it reveals more of its stronger and more controversial views about life, the universe and everything.

As you will remember from the PAC explanation, there are some fairly rigid, but conflicting opinions about which is more important to you, family or friends. The old rules of "Keep yourself to yourself"; "Keep it in the family"; "Never air your dirty linen in public"; are some of the messages given to children to enforce the belief that family is the only safe place and the only people you can trust. On the other hand there are those who grow up distrusting family and having very strong feelings and beliefs that, "You can choose your friends, but you can't choose your family"; and that, "Family would be the last people in the world I would trust, and certainly the last people I would like to spend time with!". Others, on the other hand, have learned that it is the quality of a particlar individual which makes him or her trust-worthy, not whether or not they are "family" or "friends". It is making an individual judgement about each person, family or friend that is relevant here.

The *E level* is called the *intimacy level* and is shared with one or two chosen few. This is a high risk area since you are revealing — and in some instances — demonstrating your deepest feelings and thoughts about yourself and the other person, which carries the risk of being rejected, humiliated or penalized in some way. It is the latter possibilities which lead to extreme vulnerability. The transaction level here which makes the E Level intimate is the sharing of deep feelings, thoughts, values, hope and dreams — Child to Child. The sharing on this level is probably the most sought after communication, and alas not obtained as often as people would wish it, since it implies a special relationship or bonding with another human being: Lover to Lover, Parents to Baby; Best Friend to Best Friend; Wife to Husband; Children to Parents.

The penultimate level, *Level F*, is the *self level*. These are the innermost thoughts and secrets, hopes, dreams and fantasies which are kept private to yourself. These are the things you may dream about, or your inner-most fears and worries but do not share with others. The "Three o'clock in the morning" conversations you have with yourself or perhaps with God. The inner-speculations about, "What is life all about?", "Where is all this leading to?" and "Is this all there is to life — my life?" The answers to these questions often have a high vulnerability factor if shared with others. Sometimes, even revealing the fact that you are thinking about these things is considered dangerous by others. This, we would say, is the depth of your Child; the depth of your Parent. In common sense language, it is the depth of your soul and the activity is "soul searching".

At the centre of vulnerability, and the centre of you is often a *blind spot*, as *Level G* is called. This is information that part of you has decided is too risky or painful for your conscious mind to be aware of — although at times others are aware of it by the way you act. This is usually information which carries considerable emotional pain with it, and would make you feel so vulnerable that it would put healthy functioning at risk, so you submerge it into the unconscious, unaware part of the brain.

Privacy Boundaries

Have a look at the second Bull's Eye picture. On it you will see an uneven wall around *Level C*. This is the *Privacy Boundary*. Information on the inner side is considered to be confidential and of risk to you. Information on the outside of the boundary is of lower risk and doesn't make you particularly vulnerable. Often because of the cautious nature of our culture and family philosophies, we push our privacy boundary out farther than it needs be, treating Adult informa-

68

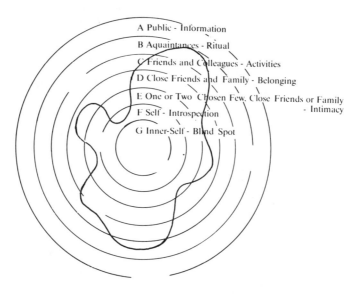

A Public - Information
B Aquaintances - Ritual
C Friends and Colleagues - Activities
D Close Friends and Family - Belonging
E One or Two Chosen Few, Close Friends or Family
    - Intimacy
F Self - Introspection
G Inner-Self - Blind Spot

Figure 16 **Privacy Boundary**

tion, and uncontroversial Parent opinions and Child likes and dislikes as extremely confidential, such as the man who says to the taxi driver's enquiry of where he wished to go, "That's none of your damned business. Just drop me on the corner of A and B Street", or the person who violently ushers the door-to-door salesman off his property because he thought the question, "Are you interested in double glazing?", an extreme violation of his personal space. Although most of us have not pushed our privacy boundaries out that far, most of us could safely reveal more about ourselves to make our lives richer and our contacts with others more varied and interesting. As the common sense saying goes — "No risk — no gain".

The Fifty-Fifty Rule

Now then, how to do this? As well as a pictorial guide to help us be more flexible and realistic in our communications with people, we can also use the Bull's Eye as a guide to how to say appropriate things to people, in the right amount, at the appropriate time and place. It's getting this right that is important. First of all, think of yourself as a notice board with the things you like on it: football, raspberries, films or real ale, for example. Activities you engage in: darts, painting, computing, video gaming, etc., and some of your thoughts and opinions.

'Think of yourself as a notice-board with the things you like on it.'

Start in the B to C Levels to make sure there is very little risk. Make an offer of one of the topics on your notice board, for example, "I went to Cornwall for my holidays last year". Wait for a response. If you get a match of the same level, then either continue with that topic—going in a bit deeper—or introduce a new topic from your notice board. Make an offer and wait for the match; if you get it, proceed. However, if you don't get it, STOP AND THINK. You have a number of choices you can make. You can make another offer going around the circle at that level; it could be that they simply did not have anything to say about the subject; or you could take a risk and take a small step in deeper, BUT ONLY ONE SMALL STEP. Or back off a step or two and initiate more from the *past-timing level*; perhaps the other person is not comfortable conversing on the level you introduced.

But whatever you do, if you don't get a match this time, don't go another step deeper. If you use this you have more options and control rather than simply discussing the weather.

Some people see the Bull's Eye as if it is a maze rather than concentric circles. Sometimes you probe around the circle at one level until you finally find the opening—that is the area you have in common and is of mutual interest—and then break through to the next level and perhaps finding the opening through to the next. When that happens you enjoy talking to the other person, and spending time with each other.

So make your offer, get a match, go sideways or deeper, and find the satisfaction that comes from talking about, or sharing something of mutual interest rather than complaining about the rain.

Steps One and Two Together
Listen to the other person and then say what you know. Again we are practising the Fifty-Fifty rule. Listening to the other person shows reasonableness, and cuts down on misunderstandings. Clearly stating your side of the picture — your thoughts, feelings, likes and dislikes, gives the other person valuable information they can use to organize their thoughts and actions. Putting Step One and Step Two together is called "CONVERSATION", and when it is done well, it is called "RAPPORT". Listen for the information the other person offers you, (sometimes called Free Information), and respond with something about you, "I" Statements or Self-Disclosure.[11] It is this give and take which establishes rapport, puts both people at ease, and ensures that the quality of information you are getting is not just superficial. An excellent guide for interviewing people is to remember to support the information people give you with something back about your experience. It doesn't have to be "deep" nor exactly matching in quantity or quality. Any little snippet which makes you a "known quantity" to the other person will ensure you get fairly reliable information from them. Otherwise it is like inviting someone to jump into a pool of water of unknown depth where there might be sharks—you of course being a potential shark. By sharing something on the other rings of your Parent and Child, they can judge that the water is shark-free and can take more risks in giving you honest answers rather than having to adapt their responses to cover themselves. One more time—remember 50/50.

EXERCISES

Bull's Eye
Level Topics: Things to say or do in each level.

Level A: Information, usually one way.
             I can give directions.
             I can tell thoughts.
             I express opinions or views in surveys but, I won't tell you
             where I live, work or what my name is.

71

Level B: Rituals

> Hello.
> How are you?
> Good to meet you.
> Nice to see you again.
> How was your journey?
> I trust you had a comfortable journey.

Level C: Activities

> What did you do last night?
> I did _____
> _____
>
> Have you completed _____ yet?
> Let's talk about the project.
> I went to _____ on holiday.
> Did you have a holiday? Where did you go?
> I played rugby/did keep-fit last Saturday (for example).
> Do you play sport?
> What kind of car do you drive?
> I have a _____ .
> My children go to _____ school.
> Fancy a drink down at the pub?
> Are you interested in Amateur Dramatics?
> I went to a play last night.
> What did you think of TV last night?
> My two-year old is not well.
> How are your children?
> My hobby is _____ .
> What's yours?

Topics of conversation

Hobbies	Work
Sport	Recreation
News	People
Children	Current events
Parents	Pubs
Homes	Geography
Pets	Education
Holidays	The Sun

Level D: Belonging Sharing opinions, likes, dislikes, time.
Report on feelings.

> What you do with your private time.
> What you like/don't like.
> What you enjoy.
> What you detest.
> What you feel/don't feel.
> Talk about love and hate.

Level E: Intimacy Sharing "private" opinions, likes, dislikes, showing feelings, sharing private time.

> Inner thoughts.
> Deep feelings.
> Hopes and dreams.
> Fears and worries.
> Expressing deep love.
> Controversial opinions.

Level F: Self

> Why am I here?
> What is the meaning of life, the universe and everything?
> What will become of me?
> Deep fears and apprehensions.

Level G: Blind spot or Buried Self

> Inner self.
> Buried fear.
> Buried pain.
> Buried hurt.

Making a Request

Step 3. State What You Want or What Action You Want Taken

This is your objective, or as the Americans would say, "The bottom line". Since Assertive behaviour is goal-oriented, Steps One and Two are there to see to it that Step Three is made as easy as possible for you and the other person. In sales terminology Step One and Two are "Opening the Sale", Step Three is "Closing the sale". As in Step Two we accomplish this by being as clear and direct as possible. Don't beat around the bush, instead of coming to the point. What we succeed in doing is arousing fear and suspicion in the other person, whereas had we come to the point, it would have been a straight-forward matter. At other times we "oversell" ourselves, i.e., not knowing when to shut up. We stay in Step 2 too long, and by the time we come to the point (Step 3), we have either bored the pants off the other person and they have lost interest, or they get annoyed that you've gone on too long. When that happens they sometimes refuse our request just to pay us back for not coming to the point.

There are some requests which automatically are difficult, particularly if the request is asking a person to do something they really do not want to do. At that point, there are a number of things to consider. Remember that being Assertive does not guarantee you will win all the time. "Win a few, lose a few". Weigh up the balance between a short term gain and a long term loss i.e.,damage to the relationship. "Is it worth it?", you ask yourself. If the answer is that you stand to lose more in the long run than you gain now, forget it. On the other hand, there are requests which we simply cannot back down from; matters to do with work or employment which may be unpleasant, but have to be done; or issues to do with our well-being or self-esteem. Since the request will have to be made, you can only make sure that you do it in the best possible way, ensuring that you do as little damage as possible.

When it comes to you and your well-being, there are a number of things that will help you. First, we have fears, sometimes called "irrational beliefs".[12] These beliefs are that if we ask someone to do something, the result will be negative. That may be true—some of the time—but not all of the time, which is why we call them irrational. They may react positively, something that never seems to occur to us. Has it occurred to you that some people consider it an honour to be asked to do things? Even if they are unpleasant tasks, most people are mature enough to know that someone has to do the job, so what's the problem? The third possible out-come is that they may be neutral, that is, have no strong feelings about it either way. We are so steeped in the philosophy of "catastrophe thinking" that we usually only entertain the negative side when making decisions about future events and what people will do. If you entertain the other two possibilities, you may find the outcome pleasantly surprising.

The Assertive Language
To state your case clearly you need a language which is as direct and as specific as possible, yet not aggressive. When making a request the words you use are "Will you...", not the demand, "Do it!", which is aggressive and Critical Parent commanding the Adapted Child. When the Adapted Child responds, there is a

50/50 chance that person will respond in the negative. Remember, Adapted Child responds in one of two ways; it complies or rebels. There is an old adage which says, "When you treat people like children, they will behave like children". When you make commands and the person complies, they will only respond with what was specifically requested — little more, since the commander has retained ownership of the problem. Sometimes, however, commands and demands are vital; to direct large numbers of people; to prevent accidents or to stop a person from doing harm. You might call these crisis interventions. Keep your demands/commands for crises because they wear out and become relatively useless for future crisis times.

Another temptation is to use, "Would you". However, "would" is hypothetical. It may only elicit feelings or "good intentions". Most of you are familiar with the old saying "I would if I could, but I can't — so I won't". Would, can also be slippery on the part of the requester. There is the sad story of the man who asked the woman, "Would you marry me?" "Yes of course", was the reply, and she promptly announced their engagement. "What did you do that for?", the man demanded to know, "Because you asked me to marry you". "No I didn't, I said *would* you marry me, meaning, I was trying to find out how you felt about me, that's all, and seeing as how I'm already married, it's quite a problem". Slippery people use a slippery language. Be straight and use will. Let people know where they stand. "Will you", of course, does not guarantee perfect success, but it does raise the odds of your getting the person to do what you ask. It seems to work for these reasons: Firstly, it gives the other person some room to manoeuvre since they have the choice of answering "yes" or "no". When people are given a choice, they are more likely to respond in the affirmative. Secondly, when you get a "yes" response, there is now an undertaking to do so; a commitment. When people give a commitment, their "yes" response, they are more likely to perform the task requested. So remember, when making a request, get a commitment.

Put it Together
Another part of the Assertive language is to link Step Two and Step Three; "I want - will you?". . . . and the describe the reasons and give the information necessary to support your request and demonstrate your reasonableness. If you say it about five times: "I want — will you", you will remember the link, and it will become automatic for your mouth to form the words. People who have the "I want — will you" approach describe it as "magic" it works so well and so easily. If you are more comfortable with a less direct approach, because sometimes the "I want — will you", seems fairly harsh, go ahead and use, "I'd like you to...", or "I'd appreciate it if..", but, end it with a "will you" to make sure you get a commitment, "I'd like you to ... so will you?"

Bad Words

Our cultural language is by nature passive. We avoid taking responsibilities for our actions. We are not only at times fearful of the direct consequences for ourselves, but fear others' judgements of us. As such, our language abounds with passive words which are said apologetically, as if we have to apologize or plead to excuse our every action with the "sorries", "ever so sorries", "if you don't minds", "I'm afraid, but", and "pleases", every other word. You don't have to plead or be apologetic because you want something from another person. It is simply a straightforward request. By the way, please and sorry are such lovely words, use them when you really mean them. Don't devalue them by using them as cover ups. Always say "Thank you". Reward what you get. It's not only courteous, it also increases the probability that that behaviour will be repeated.

We often duck our responsibilities with phrases like, "It's company policy", instead of, "I think", "The business has decided", instead of "I want" or, "It would be considered appropriate", rather than, "Will you?"

Part of the strength of Assertive behaviour is being able to demonstrate your willingness to take responsibility for your actions. People take you seriously, listen to you and are usually more willing to do what you've asked.

EXERCISES

The Assertive Language

Practise saying, "I want _____ will you", five times.

Think about the things you find it easy to ask for and put it into a "I want _____will you" sentence, and say it aloud:

"I want _____

_____

will you?"

Now think of a request you find difficult to make and put it into a "I want _____will you" sentence:

"I want _____

_____

will you?"

Now say the two requests, one after the other, the easy one first, the difficult one next, and do this *three times*.

_____

Think of a person you find it easy to ask things of. Say their name and make a "I want _____ will you" statement directed at that person: (name) _____
"I want _____
will you?"

Think of a person you find it difficult to ask, say their name and follow it with "I want _____ will you":
(name) "I want   _____

_____
will you?"
Say the two people together. The easy one first, the difficult one next, and say them aloud three times.

Make a list of the people you find it difficult to make requests of and the requests you find difficult to make. Practice them as you did above — an easy one followed by a difficult one.

People	*Requests*
_____	_____
_____	_____
_____	_____
_____	_____

CHAPTER 5
NON-VERBAL
ASSERTIVENESS

What you say, the verbal message, is only part of the process, and, as we are beginning to realise, may be of smaller importance than what we see and what we sense. The message conveyed by a person's gestures, facial expressions, head angle, arms, hands, and body posture, is called "Body Language",[13]. There has been tremendous emphasis recently in teaching people how to "decode" these indirect messages. Based on the premise that, "the media is the message", claims have been made that fairly minute details of gestures, expressions, etc., have a direct correlation with specific personal intent, or motivation. Sadly the evidence does not bear this out. What is found, however, is that *generalized* postures, gestures, and facial expressions are interpreted as indications of the behavioural mode the person is operating from, but not specific meanings to specific gestures i.e., Passive, Aggressive, or Assertive[14].

The way the visual message activates the brain is the important reason we need to be far more aware than we are of our body language. We may sound Assertive and use an Assertive language, but if our body language is incongruent — that's a lovely piece of jargon meaning "not the same as" — it will be the non-verbal message which is perceived and acted on. This can be illustrated by a French experiment[15] which demonstrated that the primitive or unconscious brain picks up visual messages which the conscious brain either is unaware of or does not see. This particular experiment was performed with a young man who was blinded at birth in one eye. One eye could see, the other was considered to be totally sightless and was proved so by all ordinary tests. However, it was not the eye which was damaged, nor the optical nerve, it was the part of the brain where visual messages are translated into conscious awareness and thought. An experiment was set up to see if any other part of the brain was receiving visual messages even though the thinking brain was not. A patch was placed over the man's "blind eye", and lights flashed on a wall. He was asked to say if he saw the light and where. As expected, he could see it and say where it had flashed. His "good" eye was covered and the lights flashed once more. This time as expected, he reported seeing no lights, nothing. Once more the lights were flashed, but this time the young man was given a stick and asked to point to the place where he thought the lights may have flashed. Nine times out of ten, over 100 trials, he pointed to the correct position on the wall! The conclusions of this study were that the primitive brain was "seeing" and directing behaviour — the arm moving the pointer — without the conscious brain "seeing" or being aware that the primitive brain had picked up and acted on the visual messages!

As you will recall from the brain model, the primitive brain is responsible for the "feeling" behaviours, Passive and Aggressive, while the higher brain is responsible for thinking and problem solving. How many times have you said, "I don't know why, but I just have an uneasy feeling about the man", even though there is nothing you can put your finger on, or the person has not said anything that sounded out of line. Have you ever felt yourself becoming tense and anxious during a conversation, although the verbals sounded OK? It works the other way round as well. A person can look calm and reassuring, and even though the verbal message is unpleasant, you seem to trust them. If the way you look at people can have such an effect on them or the outcome of the situation, and maybe even the relationship, then it is important to be aware of your body and how you look to others. Remember, it is not how *you* think you look that is important, it is how *others* perceive you. Your objective will be to get the two things in line, or congruent, so how you wish to be seen is the way you are seen.

Passive Posturing
MOTIVATING ATTITUDE: Inferior
MOTIVATING FEELING: Fear, anxiety
BODY POSTURE: Closed position; or, Turning away from; or, Curled up.
LEGS AND FEET: *Standing*: Unsteady on feet; or, Shifting weight from one foot to the other. Standing with weight on one foot. Rolling foot over on the side of the ankle, or, Moving up and down on the balls of the feet. Wobbly knees.
Sitting: Legs curled one around the other.
ARMS & HANDS: Folded tightly across the body; or Hands in pockets. Hand covering mouth; or Hand on back of neck; or Hands tightly clasped; or Hands fidgeting with pen, paperclips, etc.; or twisting handkerchief; or biting fingernails, or Wringing hands.
HEAD: Bowed or Cocked at an angle; Turned away.
EYE CONTACT: Avoids direct eye contact totally; or, Quick furtive glances; or Looks down; or Eyes dart from side to side while speaking.
FACIAL EXPRESSION: Worried; or Tense; or Frowns; or Grimaces; or Bites lips; or Bites inside of cheeks; or Flattened cheek muscles; or Pale colour; or Blushing.
BREATHING PATTERN: Shallow and irregular; or Holding breath; or Deep

79

sighs; or Audible gasps.

BODY ODOUR: presence of strong body odour called "Smell of Fear" if very worried or tense; or Perspires easily and readily.

Aggressive Posturing

MOTIVATING ATTITUDE: Superiority or Defence against Inferior.

MOTIVATING FEELINGS: Anger, tension.

BODY POSTURE: Closed, arms folded across chest in a disapproving manner; or as if to hold back anger. Maybe leaning forward or moving forward in an intimidating or attacking position.

LEGS AND FEET: *Standing*: Moving forward; or Belligerently entrenched. *Sitting*: Foot tapping or repetitive foot swinging.

ARMS & HANDS: Folded across chest; or Hands on hips, or Hand and arm raised in a lecturing position; or Fists on hips; or Hands clinched tightly to form fist; or Tightly held togther to hold onto anger; or Index finger (Critical Parent finger) extended in pointing or jabbing position.

HEAD: Forward or Chin forward.

EYE CONTACT: Hard eye contact; or Staring; or Narrowing of the eyes; or Unblinking; or Looking past or through the person.

FACIAL EXPRESSION: Jaw set; or Teeth clenched, or Muscles taut; or Facial colouring turning red; or Sometimes when very angry, turning white.

BREATHING PATTERN: Audible intake of breath; or Breathing rate faster; or Sucking in air through teeth.

BODY ODOUR: Not noticeable unless the aggression is covering fear.

Assertive Posturing

MOTIVATING ATTITUDE: You and I are equals.

MOTIVATING FEELING: Well-being; or Excitement; or Fun; or Calm.

BODY POSTURE: Open. Arms comfortably by sides; or One hand in pocket; or Hands and arms behind back; or Hands clasped together in front of body; or Attentive; or Calm; or Relaxed but Alert.

LEGS AND FEET: *Standing*: Feet about shoulder width apart with weight equally distributed on both feet. Standing still.

Sitting: Both feet on the floor. One leg crossed over the other (once). Still.

ARMS: *Standing*: See body posture.

Sitting: Resting on arm or arms of chair, or on lap.

HANDS: Comfortably resting by side, or Folded comfortably on lap, or Still not fidgeting.

HEAD: Straight forward facing person. Level.

EYE CONTACT: Looking at person. Eyes resting comfortably on face, or

Direct eye contact, or Looking away but coming back and looking at other person.
FACIAL EXPRESSION: Calm. Facial muscles relaxed. Smile — but not a grin. Normal face colouring.
BREATHING PATTERN: Regular.
BODY ODOUR: No strong odours.

There is no such things as a "Bad" behaviour. There is a time and place for all three. Practice so you can move from one behavioural stance to another with ease. Also, practise is the only way to programme your brain to instantly recognise which behavioural operating system you are using.

EXERCISES

Body Language
1.   Stand in front of a mirror and practise the three body stances: Passive, Aggressive, Assertive.
      See pages 79-81 for description.
2.   When you have practised the three postures, move from one to another as quickly as possible, but make sure you change all of your body, and your facial expressions.
      Passive   Aggressive
      Aggressive   Assertive
      Passive   Assertive
      Assertive   Aggressive
      Aggressive   Passive

3.   Find a person who will watch you and give you feedback. Ask them to tell you which posture you are portraying and what to do to make each one more convincing.

Reading Body Language
When you are watching TV, turn down the sound and watch the actors' and actresses' body language and facial expressions. Try to guess what they are feeling and saying by the way they look, their facial expressions and gestures.

Practice:
Private: Next, if it is possible, Practise imitating their gestures, expressions and body posture.

Public: In a public place, such as public transport, trains, buses etc., watch the body language of people you see there. Look at their facial expressions and gestures, body postures, and if possible imitate *some* of the gestures, expressions and posturings.

Meetings: In a meeting, choose two people to observe, one who is speaking and one who is listening. See what feelings or attitudes the speaker is portraying non-verbally and what effect it has on the listeners.

Watch: Watch someone who is listening. Guess what they are thinking and what they will say by watching their facial expressions, posture etc.

One thing I learnt was _____

_____

_____

'Stand in front of a mirror and practise the three body stances; Passive, Aggressive, and Assertive.'

CHAPTER 6
VERBAL ASSERTION:
Part Two

Saying No

Now that you have learned to ask for things, how do you say "no" to people who ask you to do things which you don't want to, or can't do. It's a strange thing, this "No" word. If you use it you are labelled by others, or learn to consider yourself, as negative, uncooperative and unfriendly. "No", seems to be the ultimate bad word, and to avoid using it we learn to lie. We lie in two ways. We learn to make up all kinds of lies — called excuses — rather than come out with a "No". Or we say "Yes", when what we'd really like to say is "No" and then forget about it, or complete the task in a rush so it's not adequately done, or show up late, or take on so much that our life is in a frenzy and we collapse from exhaustion or die of stress. You are then labelled undependable and unreliable — but it still seems preferable to be deemed unreliable or to die of a stress disease, than to say "No".

Have a look at it in a different light. Here you are, walking around in your own little world, minding your own business, when this person *chooses* to come into your world and make a request. You didn't invite them, they chose to enter your world. Now, if you say "No", you are suddenly a "bad person". It doesn't make sense, does it?

It is not suggested that you say "No" all the time, that really would make you uncooperative and negative. What is being suggested is to weigh it up. If it's OK to say "Yes", then say "Yes". If *your* priorities come first, look at your list of rights, then say "No". "But what if the reaction from the other person is so terrible that I have to give in?" That may be true, others may not like your saying no and react angrily. If that should happen, there are a number of things that you can do:-
1. Stay calm.
2. Don't argue back.
3. Use techniques, such as "Broken Record" to stay with your "No". Also, you really aren't as fragile as you think you are. After all, anger or verbal aggression

is only words. It is not a threat to you physically, so they really can't hurt you. Keep telling yourself that, "It's only words".

Sometimes we fear the opposite, that is, if we say "No", the other person will fall apart; they will be so hurt and devastated. Part of the time, that could be true. "No" seems to people a rejection of them as a person. If that should happen, you can still say "No", but with kindness and understanding; giving assurance to the person that you are not rejecting them, simply because you have said "No" to a request. Most of the time, however, people are stronger than you think they are, and they see "No" simply as a refusal to a request, and then get on with their business. Change your way of viewing people — and yourself. Give some credit to others and yourself for strength of character.

Another positive factor in saying "No", is that not only does it make you a reliable person, it gives others the information they need to organise their priorities and structure their time. If you say "No" when you mean no, and "Yes" when you mean yes, people know where they stand with you. How often have you heard the phrase, "Some decision is better than no decision". The same is true for No. A No is better than a Yes when the Yes is untrue or unreliable.

When you say "No", don't just give the short sharp "No" or "The answer is no" and that's all. That is aggressive and will more than likely raise hackles. Give some information, explain your reasons. Tell them why. You are more likely to have your no accepted and, although the other person maybe disappointed, they are not likely to be too unhappy with you, and the relationship stays intact. However, there are, as with making a request, some ways which are better than others to accomplish this.

Assertive Language for No
As you will recall, the specific language for making a request is "Will you?". Saying "No" is the opposite, "I won't". That sometimes appears harsh, so be sure to soften it with plenty of information in Step Two. "These are the reasons why — x,y,z — so no I won't". Often our temptation is to say, "I can't", which can be interpreted as an excuse. That's a set up for a game which goes — "If I can get around all of your excuses, then you have got to give in", or "Why don't you—a, b, c?" "I can't because". However, there are times, real constraints which inhibit you from doing something. You really cannot. When that is the case, say your "I can't" and give your reasons why, and follow it with, "So, No, I won't". That puts the finish on it so people know that it is not an invitation to play the "Why don't you?" game.

A point to remember: Make sure you actually say "No". Possibly because we find that word so distasteful we avoid saying it. Yet it is very clear and to the point. Women in particular not only seem to say it, but act as if they don't know how to say it. They, in particular, have learned the trick of saying "No" and "Yes" at the same time. How they do that is to say the word "No" and nod their head "Yes". The head movement for "No" is from side to side. Try it. If it is difficult then practise it when you are sitting on your own. When you are saying "No", make a point of getting your head shake in as well as saying the word. You will be surprised how definite this makes you appear and how seriously people take you.

More Bad Words
The passive words which appeared in the previous bad word list are also applied to "No". Usually we try to couch the "No" in a sheath of "I'm afraids", "I'm ever so sorry but", and lots of sighing and inhaling through our teeth. Nonsense. What are you sorry about? What are you afraid of? "No" is simply a negative response to a request for a behavioural act. Nothing more, nothing less.

EXERCISES

Say No (Talk out loud)
Requests or orders I would like to say "No" to, but don't, are:

_____

_____

One request I find easy to say "No" to is: _____

_____

One person I find it easy to say "No" to: _____

_____

The Assertive language for saying "No" is, "I can't because" (list the reasons why you can't comply with the request).

_____

_____

_____

Now say your "No" using the Assertive language to the person it is easy to say "No" to, then say "No" to the person who is difficult. Say it three times.
(name of easy person) _____

_____

I can't do that, so "No" I won't.
(name of difficult person) _____

_____

I can't do that, so "No" I won't.
Repeat the two together three times.

Are you having difficulty finding someone you *could* say "No" to? If so, think of a child you could say "No" to — or an animal — the dog, the cat, the goldfish, or if that isn't possible, start with inanimate objects such as a door, a lamp-post, people on TV, etc, and work your way up to the difficult people.

No to Difficult Requests
Say outloud something you find easy to say "No" to.
Example (easy) "I don't like lending my records, so "No" I won't."

Now say something you find difficult to say "No" to.
Example (difficult) "I cannot see this client tomorrow as much as I would like to, I have too much work to finish, so "No" I won't".

Easy: I can't because _____

_____ so "No" I won't

Difficult: I can't because _____

_____ so "No" I won't

Repeat three times

Practise each difficult situation in the same way — easy first, difficult second. Repeat three times.

Caution: Always start with the easy situations and easy people to say "No" to. Tackle the difficult situations when you have built up your skill and confidence.

Remember, you have the right to be in charge of your life, to put yourself first — sometimes, and to do so you need to be able to say "No" from time to time. Not to everything, and not to all people, but from time to time.

Saying No or Making Your Request in the Face of Strong Manipulation

Sometimes we encounter people who do not respond to our straightforward requests or to our "Nos", no matter how firm they may be. There are people in the world, who for a number of reasons, are determined to get their own way regardless of the circumstances or your wants or needs; or who either do not share your value systems or ignore them. These people either may be in an extreme emotional state, or extremely selfish, or been trained not to respond to your wishes, or have a personality which is deficient of social norms and standards. When faced with these kinds of people you have to know a few tricks to prevent them from manipulating you, and in the extreme, to stay OK around them. One of the techniques is to think ahead: "What do you want from the encounter?". Have a goal in mind, and then say your *Step Three Phrase* and persistently stick to it. It may be a request, or it may be a "No". Whichever it is, keep coming back to it, and saying it each time you do your Listen and Tell Steps. In some cases, people use their gift of language and their eloquent tongues to tie you in knots and confuse you; if you try to follow their reasoning or try to reason with them, you often find yourself turned inside out, hopelessly confused and helplessly give in. If you keep your goal in mind, and keep remembering to persistently come back to your *Step 3 Phrase*—no matter where the argument leads you—you can hold on to what you want without being forced into aggression or hopelessly losing your way and your courage, and giving up.

1. *You do not have to answer a question.*

Think about it. Why should you have to respond to every Tom, Dick and Harry who comes along and asks you a question? Perhaps it was true when you were a child and were taught to respond to adults when they spoke to you or questioned you, but you are no longer a child and do not have to behave in that child-like manner. A ploy that manipulative people use is to ask trick or trapping questions: "Do you always behave in this way?", implying that by not doing what the other person wants, you are an undesirable person, and of course doing what the other person wants says you lose. That's called, "Heads I win, tails you lose". "When did you stop beating your wife?", is the classic of this kind of question. It's, "you lose no matter how you answer". That's called a "double bind". You certainly know it is a bind, because you are the person caught in it. Some politicians are masters of this kind of dialogue. To avoid being trapped or put in a bind, either don't answer the question or answer what you want the person to hear—which may not be a direct answer to the question.

2. *You do not have to wait to be given an opportunity to respond.*

As we have learned previously, a conversation is a two-way process. That happens, however, when both parties respect each other to some degree and are willing to give and take. When you are dealing with someone who is highly manipulative that is not the case. Talk when you have something you want to say or something you want them to hear. Interrupt, or in the extreme, if they will not give you a space to talk, talk even if it means talking at the same time. Again, you can do so without being aggressive or rude.

3. *If you wish to be heard, talk softer not louder than the other person.*
Sometimes when someone is in "full flight", and won't stop talking, or simply ignores your attempts to get your point across, the temptation is to talk louder to make yourself heard. That leads to their talking louder, you yelling, them yelling, and can end in a screaming match, which can dangerously lead to, "words uttered in the heat of the moment to be regretted later"; or at other times to physical violence. In this situation, try the opposite. Talk softer. Not terribly soft, but just under their volume level and calmly keep repeating your point or your Step 3 Phrase. Because humans are by nature curious animals, you will find that they stop talking to hear what you are saying. Going a step lower often has better results than going a step higher. Even if you find that you have forgotten yourself and find you have risen to the bait, Stop. Calm down., Soften your voice. Stop arguing and use your *Broken Record Phrase*, until the other person becomes reasonable, listens to you, or stops.

EXERCISE

Let's practise persistence using a Broken Record technique. Decide what your Bottom Line phrase will be.

Example: "No I won't go with you."
              or, "Stop that,"
              or, "Will you leave."

To begin with, get your phrases clearly in mind by saying your BR phrase aloud five times. Then practise with a partner. Have a partner say anything he or she wants to you, and you give your BR response.

When you practise your BR technique,
Practice:
Interrupting with it.
Talking at the same time.
Smiling and talking.
Talking louder.
Talking softer.
Practise shaking your head "No" if you are using a "No" phrase.
And nodding your head "Yes" if you are making a request.
This one needs another person to practise with. If you cannot find a person, use the TV. Be prepared to laugh a lot. Turn into a quiz or news programme, and talk to the people on the TV, practising your BR phrase on him/her.

'Stop arguing and use your broken record phrase', until the other person becomes reasonable, listens to you or stops.

Workable Compromise

What happens when one assertive person meets another assertive person — both prepared to stick to their guns and neither backing down. At that point you move to a compromise position. Make a note, however, that it is *only* after you have pushed the limits that you go into this arena. Here is a guide as to how to set up the compromise. Notice it is called *workable* compromise, not fair compromise. Compromise is not necessarily fair because someone or both of you ends up having to give up something. The Child part of us usually believes that giving up something you want is not fair. Because of that, we find it difficult and often sabotage or undermine the compromise process if it is fairness we are aiming for. We can side step that if we aim for "workable" instead. Even so, we still have to do a check to see if enough of the "fairness" is left in to satisfy the Child so that it does not engage in guerilla warfare in order to get some of its "own back". Have a look at the guide to Workable Compromise.[16]

Person A		Person B
STEP 1	This is what I want. What do you want?	This is what I want.
STEP 2	This is what I'm prepared to give up to get most of what I want. What are you prepared to give up?	This is what I am prepared to give up.
STEP 3	This is how I feel. How do you feel?	This is how I feel.

Table II
Workable Compromise

There are some things to consider before you use this formula. First of all do not do so unless you have the other person's agreement that they will be straightforward and direct. If you do not, that will be very naive of you to the point of stupidity. Never play show and tell unless the other person has agreed to play show and tell. If you don't, and show all, you may well be caught in a very embarassing or detrimental position. Once you do have their agreement to be direct, you may wish to hold back a little to probe to see if they will honour that agreement. Remember the 50-50 Rule? Well, you apply it here. Don't put all of your cards on the table first go. Show a few, and if you get a match back, show some more. Go somewhat cautiously before stating everything you are prepared to give up.

Step One is straightforward. It is the crystallization of the 1-2-3 Steps for Assertively Making a Request or Saying "No". When you see that you have reached an inflexible situation, you move to Step Three which is to offer a compromise. It is often important to recognize when enough is enough and it is time to move on. If you hold on in an entrenched position, you may find that someone else will step in and take the decision making process out of your hands. Sometimes we think that that is a realistic step, having an arbiter. And sometimes that is true; there are deadlocks which do need some influence from the outside to get things moving again. However, whenever we do that we put our fate in the hands of people who will use their own value system to make judgements about us and for us, *and their priorities may not be our priorities.* You actually stand a better chance if you responsibly, for the sake of getting on and/or getting the job done, offer to give a little on your position. But remember it is only as much as the other person is prepared to give. If you practise the 50-50 Rule you should come out OK, losing the bare minimum in order to get on.

Step 5. *This is how I feel, how do you feel?* is the safeguard to make sure we have kept a balance between the two parties on the giving up or giving in. You won't feel happy or over the moon because you have just had to give up something which you obviously wanted or you wouldn't have put so much energy into trying to get it. In fact you may feel unhappy or disappointed. The point here is to share this feeling of disappointment equally between you. If one person feels particularly hard done by, watch out because they will then enter into the "get-even phase", often behind your back. Check to see if you share approximately the same share of dissatisfaction or unhappiness. If you do, OK. If you don't, go back to the beginning and renegotiate until you have a balanced feeling outcome.

Some people think that the person who starts first has the power position since they may pre-empt the hand of the other. Others think differently, saying that the second person has the better position because he/she has been able to see what the other person is willing to do. There probably is no "right" answer to this. It is simply a matter of personal preference. Also remember there is no rule written anywhere that you only have one chance. Renegotiate as many times as you wish.

EXERCISES

STEP ONE: Clearly state your side of the case and give your reasons.
Don't move to Step Two until you are sure you cannot achieve your objective.
PERSON A: This is what I want. _____
_____
_____
_____

PERSON B: This is what I want. _____
_____
_____
_____

Now take a red pencil or pen and encircle the areas where you are in conflict.

STEP TWO: This is what I'm prepared to give up to get the most of what I want.
PERSON A: _____

_____

_____

PERSON B: _____

_____

_____

Repeat Step Two as many times as is necessary to come to a workable agreement.

STEP THREE: This is how I feel (angry, irritated, upset, OK, pleased).
PERSON A: _____

_____

_____

PERSON B: _____

_____

_____

If you don't both feel equally OK about what has been decided, then you haven't achieved a Workable Compromise. Someone has won too much. Go back and renegotiate until the feelings match.

Go through the negotiation process several times looking for different solutions, so you have a number to choose from.

CHAPTER 7
NON-VERBAL
PRESENTATION

Eye Contact

Much has been said about the importance of eye contact. As a child you are yelled at for not looking at people when they talk to you, and are told stories about the "Shifty-eyed" people who don't look people in the eye because they are dishonest. However, when you do, you are told off for staring, because it is rude, another of those Parent double binds. If eye contact weren't so powerful, it wouldn't be given such importance. Passive people are afraid of it; Aggressive people overuse it in an attempt to dominate or humiliate; Assertive people know that it is a major key to personal power.

If you have ever tried to look someone in the eyes for any prolonged period of time, you know the power involved: your eyes start to water. As experience tells us, the feeling link between people takes place through eye contact. Picture the gazes between two people who love each other and how the message of love is conveyed through the meeting of gazes. At the other end of the feeling's continuum is the strong negative feeling of hatred and anger, and how adequately that is conveyed by hard aggressive stares. On the more ordinary level, sensing how the other person is feeling or what they are thinking happens with eye contact. Who was it that said "eyes are the window of the soul"? Eye contact is the invisible bridge between people which carries the feeling, intuitive level of communication.

As well as carrying the feeling level of communication, making eye contact makes you a better listener, as noted in Chapter Three. You actually take in more by looking in a level, straightforward position[9], which means looking at the person in front of you who is talking to you. Try it for yourself. When you look away you will see how your attention drifts, you become distracted by other things, and you find you are listening to your own thoughts rather than what is being told to you, and in general you do not hear as well.

Now to deal with the problems of the double bind, a damned if you do and a damned if you don't predicament. Because we have been told so many times

93

that it is rude to stare, or that the only times we remembered getting eye contact was the hard shot of an angry stare when we had been bad. Now we neither know how to make eye contact nor receive eye contact in a comfortable way. Here are a few tips to help you. Every person has a blind spot; a place where you could rest your gaze for a long period of time and the person would not be aware that you were not looking directly at him or her. In general you can be quite sure of hitting it if you rest your gaze on the other person's *eye brows, tip of the nose, or bridge of the nose*. But be sure you come back and re-establish eye contact every now and then, because although the other person will not see you are not looking directly at him/her, they will eventually sense it or feel it.

Use the same guide for receiving eye contact, particularly from a person who is angry, dominating or critical. You will find you can protect your vulnerability by diluting the intensity of their stare, while remaining calm and Assertive. There was one woman who used this with her boss who was an extremely critical and sarcastic man. Although she quite liked him, she was very afraid of his criticisms. She found that she could face him, smile and listen calmly to his criticisms because she had practised the blindspot technique and actually carried it a step further. When she knew she was facing a heavy session of criticism, she would take her contact lenses off before going in to see him. She says work has never been better!

'How to get eye contact.'

Catching Their Eye

Know the importance of eye contact; what to do if you can't get people to look at you when you talk to them, or if you are trying to interrupt in order to talk to them. Do you passively sit there, politely waiting and then forget what it was you wanted to say since you waited so long, or walk away and say "Oh, why bother?"? The Aggression approach is to use phrases like, "If you don't mind...". "You can't get a word in edgewise around here", or "Look sunshine, look at me when I am talking to you", or bang the table. The Assertive approach is more subtle. It needs to be effective, because, although you want the person to look at you, you don't want to be seen as pushy and domineering. Here's some ideas to use to get people to look at you. If you are very good at it, they won't even notice what you have done — so the key word is SUBTLETY. These interventions are listed in order of least powerful to most powerful.

How to get Eye Contact

Least powerful	*MOVEMENT*: with Hand, Head, Body
	SOUND: Make a sound. Say their name.
	Ask a question.
	Absence of sound.
Most powerful	*TOUCH*: Lightly on the arm or shoulder.

Movement

Movement works to attract visual attention because Mother Nature programmed our brains way back when, with that survival mechanism. If you did not see movement in the jungle or the plains, you didn't live very long, because the movement you missed may have been a predator and you were its next meal; or the movement came from your next meal and you died of starvation because you didn't see it. Although we seldom operate on that level today, we still have this movement detector working — and now we can put it to use to meet present-day situations.

The most unobtrusive of the movements to make is to move your hand. Since most people make hand gestures, it isn't very noticeable when you deliberately try to attract a person's attention by moving your hand. A bright pen or shiny object will often help capture attention. When you have it, move your hand up near your face and make eye contact. If the person looks past you, or has their head to one side, you can easily lean your head over to one side, capture their

95

visual attention, carry on talking, and as you straighten up they should follow. If you have someone who does not respond to either of these, then get up and move until you are standing opposite that person, or to the spot where that person looks. How about the person who looks down while you are talking to them? Well, everyone has accidents from time to time. Drop something on the floor, and as you bend down to pick it up, make eye contact from the floor and continue your conversation from there. However, you can't stay down there forever, and you can't keep dropping things on the floor, so it is perhaps best to save that one for the most important message you want this person to hear.

Think of movement in this way. You are a conductor, conducting the communication flow called conversation. If you are dealing with a group of people you can get people to look at you and listen to you simply by making a few movements, attracting eye contact from all the group, or different people at a time, and if you do it well, they will not notice anything out of the ordinary.

WATCH POINT:

There is an important point to watch here. Because movement detection is an automatic process, it sets off the alarm system whenever a movement is detected. No matter what we are doing, our cognitive brain has a slight pause while it investigates the source of the danger. It can proceed with the cognitive function it was engaged in only after investigating the cause of the movement by a glance, pause, etc. Can you remember what it is like trying to talk, reason, argue or negotiate when someone in the room — not even necessarily the person you were talking to, was making a repeated movement, jiggling their foot, tapping their fingers or waving a pencil around? Constantly your primitive brain is overriding your cognitive brain with a danger warning. "Danger, Danger, Danger, sabre tooth tiger lurking behind that desk". You cannot turn off this mechanism. You may succeed in diminishing it, but you can't ignore it totally. How hard it is then to concentrate or talk when someone is making these agitated movements. No wonder the thing that drives teachers bananas is kids squirming at their desks.

Sound

Sound is next on the list. The attraction now becomes more intense and less subtle. Sound, like movement, is part of the natural surveillance system nature gave us for protection. "What was that sound in the forest?", or "Why has that sound stopped?", a warning sign of danger, and, like movement, very difficult to ignore. Hear a sound, and you look up or around you to see what it is. Here are some sounds to use to get attention; close a book, move your chair, clear your throat, cough, make a comment, they are all natural sound interrupters.

Our cultural and educational upbringings have trained us to be polite and answer all questions asked; plus the rememberance of school days when you were caught miles away in a day-dream, keeps people looking at you and alert if you direct a question at them. Add to that the family electrodes of saying their name and you have their undivided attention. Remember being in a crowded and noisy place and hearing your name even though no one else heard it?

Absence of sound works, as said, in the same way. If you are speaking and not getting the other person's attention, stop talking, they'll soon look up. When you are speaking, speak loudly enough for the other person to hear, vary the cadence, the pitch and the tempo enough to make the sound patterns different and interesting. Speak at the same tempo in lowish tones, and you will put the other person to sleep. Well it should, because that is how people are put into a trance in hypnosis.

WATCH POINT
Because sound, like movement, is an alarm system, the repetitive sounds of agitation have the same effect on a person's thinking, talking or concentrating. The drumming of fingers on a table top, the constant clicking of the tops of ball point pens, sends the toughest person round the twist. A fairly predictable response is to erupt angrily, and usually no one can understand why. The energy required to keep the cognitive part of the brain operating in face of the bombardment from the primitive brain's danger warnings is draining, tiring and trying.

Touch
The third and most powerful attention getter and interrupter is touch. Touch is the first and most powerful recognition you receive as a very young child. It tells you you are alive and wanted[17]. It carries some of that power with it always. Studies have demonstrated that you can get people to tell the truth, influence their perceptions of people and organizations, and influence their perceptions of having a good day and bad day[19]. With something that powerful, it has to be used carefully. A problem with touch in some cultures, the English culture in particular, is that it is not OK for people to touch. If a man were to touch another man, he would have his sexuality suspected, and these days, if a man were to touch a woman, he would be done for sexual harassment. To use touch and make sure neither happens, the question of where to touch is important. In general the safe areas of the body are arms, upper arms and shoulders. The objective for touch is to be so brief and light that the other person isn't aware they have been touched. If you are still concerned about the intimacy that touching might convey, use the back of your hand, instead of the front, or touch

97

with an object such as a sheet of paper or a pencil. However, if you do use an object, make sure you touch the person with it and not hit them or poke them with it.

Some people do not like to be touched. These people were probably raised in a home where touching and other displays of feelings did not happen or was ridiculed. You can usually tell who these people are because they back off when you walk near them; sit in the farthest corner of the chair, sometimes turning away from people. They become perceptibly agitated if touched, and if you persist, will try to avoid you. If you wish to use touching to capture their attention you must be very subtle. Touching them with an object, such as a sheet of paper, is usually OK, but if it isn't, then don't touch. It creates a great deal of discomfort for them and problems for you, and it will change their perceptions of you to negative rather than positive.

EXERCISE

Practicing Eye Contact

First of all practise looking at people's faces and training yourself to remember what you see. Since this usually is taken as a sign of "interest", practise in an uninvolved way. Look at the faces of people on television. Then close your eyes and practise what they look like.

What colour hair?	Beard?
What colour eyes?	Shape of nose?
Glasses?	Shape of face?

Second

Look at faces in a crowd or in a meeting. Let your gaze wander around the faces of people there. Turn your eyes away and recall what they look like. Turn back, and this time look at the person's eyebrows, forehead, cheeks, nose, and lips. See how long you can do this.

Third

As you hold a conversation with someone, make eye contact. If you are fairly close to the person, look at one eye then the other, shifting back and forward to avoid "staring".

To make eye contact more comfortable, look at the bridge of the nose, tip of the nose, eyebrows and mouth, but remember to come back from time to time and re-establish direct eye contact.

CHAPTER 8
PROTECTION SKILLS I

Blocks to Assertive Behaviour: Anxiety

The mechanism which creates the largest block to doing things we would like to do, and saying the things we would like to say is anxiety. If you will have a look at the diagram on this page, you will see that anxiety blocks our plans for Assertive Behaviour, and almost automatically ensures that we respond with one of the Feeling Behaviours: Passive or Aggressive. It is anxiety which pushes the button to operate the primitive part of the brain and shuts down the cognitive or thinking brain. What causes the anxiety buttons to be pushed are bad experiences and the Internal Parent dialogue which threatens us to "Get it right this time", and "Don't make a fool of yourself". That, of course, is an iron-clad method to ensure you will become so tense and anxious that you do mess it up.

To understand this have a look at how the anxiety mechanism operates. Perhaps you can recall from Chapter One, we said that built inside every human being is a striving for health: physical and emotional. Anxiety is the mechanism which activates this striving. Look at Figure 17 and you will see how this is accomplished.

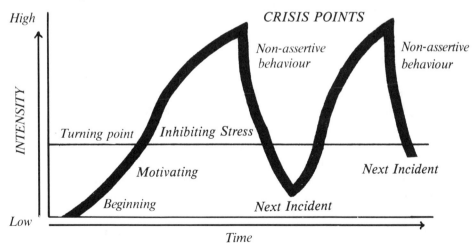

Figure 17
Effects of Anxiety on Behaviour

99

To begin with, anxiety is the command to the brain that some part of the person, either body or mind, is in a state of imbalance. At that level, we say anxiety is a motivator, a signal to the brain to command the body to do something to relieve the discomfort. If ignored, the anxiety builds up, increasing tension and worry to a point where it becomes too uncomfortable and no longer functions as a motivator but becomes an inhibitor. Now we have a loop which keeps repeating itself: worry leading to more tension and anxiety, and more tension and anxiety leading to further inaction and further worry. Finally, the safety mechanism takes over. That is called crisis point on the diagram, and then one of the non-thinking behaviours is enacted: Passive Behaviour to get us out of, or away from the problem—in the extreme this Passive Behaviour is called depression—or else Aggressive Behaviour to do something to move the problem away from us. All of us have had some experience in one kind of this Anxiety build up. It is called "delay" or "putting off" — until finally we can wait no longer. Then we erupt in a flurry of activity, burning the midnight oil, etc. Why this type of activity is classed Aggressive Behaviour is that everyone is expected to drop what they are doing, mobilize around the active person, and forget their own priorities. At the end of the hyperactive period of crisis, the phrase that is usually uttered by most of us is, "If only I had organized my time better, I could have done a much better job".

This concept of anxiety build-up culminating in crisis, can also be used to explain how "cashing in stamps" works. As you put each stamp in your stamp book, you do yourself some harm, and build anxiety and frustration. When you have enough, i.e., the anxiety level is too uncomfortable, the natural cut-off mechanism takes over and you get rid of the lot, a kind of catharsis.

Managing Anxiety

Anxiety in small doses is not bad. It provides some spice and excitement to life. It puts some zest into what would ordinarily be a humdrum existence. Performers, before they appear on stage, get themselves "keyed up" to improve the spirit and quality of their performance. The same is true for all people. Some anxiety is exciting, fun and stimulating. Too much prohibits us from doing the things we would really like to do in life, and sometimes turns into stress diseases which are often disabling and sometimes fatal. There are at least two areas to tackle which can help reduce anxiety from the harmful inhibiting level to the exciting and creative level. One is to give yourself good, encouraging Parent messages, and stop or block the old worrying or guilt inducing messages. The other, is to learn to relax.

"You Can Do It, Messages"

Many of the things told to you when you were a child by your parents were actually said in your best interests, or so your parents thought. What parents don't realise is how ill-equipped the immature child's brain is to sort out and classify "Why who said what". Kids swallow it whole. When said to a child, "We Smiths are all alike", the Smith child incorporates everything he knows about being a Smith. "Be careful messages" may be protective at the time, but they effectively inhibit the child from trying new things and being creative or adventurous. "Be the Best" means, "If you can't be best, don't do anything"; and "Don't be stupid" makes the assumption that you already are stupid otherwise they wouldn't have told you not to be in the first place. The same as "Get it right" messsages imply that you are obviously not getting it right otherwise they wouldn't have had to warn you about getting it right. All these serve to limit and check a person's spontaneous behaviour, creativity and enthusiasm. They do not encourage him or her. It is your parents talking to you inside your head with these kinds of messages which creates the build up of your anxiety. Today we normally call it "worry".

To cut across this worry syndrome, replace the old rubbish with some new encouraging slogans for yourself. Get to be your own best friend. Tell yourself the following:

1.   "Come on, you can do it."
2.   "If at first you don't succeed, keep at it until you do."
3.   "What's worth doing at all is worth doing."
4.   "You are as bright and capable as most people."
5.   "You are not a robot." "You are a human and therefore not perfect."
6.   "You will make mistakes and learn from them."
7.   "Win a few, lose a few."
8.   "Well done."
9.   "You did it." "I knew you could."
10. "Hurrah!!!"

Relaxation

A way we can actually dampen anxiety is to practise some form of relaxation. Relaxation comes in many forms. Sitting down and unwinding after a day of mental or physical activity; spending time socially with people we enjoy, either friends or family; playing your favourite sport, a night out with the girls or with the boys, unwinding in front of the television or sleeping. What has been found, however is that with our ever increasing pace of life, some of the more traditional methods of relaxation don't fill the bill. They don't get rid of the residue of anxiety and tension which accumulates. Some people have

101

mistakenly believed they have solved the problem by participating in an exhausting sport such as squash or handball, or swimming laps against the clock or running. This does not help the body relax, it exhausts the body. It is not the sport which is at fault, it is the way some people use it. It is thrashing yourslf to exhaustion which is the fault. You think that it is relaxing because you have used up excess nervous tension (anxiety), but you are really adding to the damage by requiring an already fatigued body to drive harder. Sleep also doesn't always help because sometimes you are too wound up to get to sleep. Most of you, unfortunately, have had the experiences of being so tense that you have actually had it wake you up, or woken up in the morning, knowing you have had a night's sleep, but feeling as if you have walked a hundred miles. That's because, sometimes we hold too much tension in our bodies to relax enough to get rid of it all through sleep. Then there are those times when you either can't get to sleep or awaken in the middle of the night, usually with the early dawn chorus, and can't get back to sleep. The harder you try, the more tense and upset you become.

What we look at today are forms of relaxation which directly aim at shutting off the mind and relaxing the body. Meditation is one way. Relaxation response and self-hypnosis are others. Meditation has been around for many centuries, as people mostly of the Eastern cultures have sought to find peace of mind and answers to life, the universe and everything. However, used in our Western culture, meditation is not particularly healthy, in fact for a certain group of people, men over 40, is actually harmful, *if it is not linked to some kind of problem solving.*[3] If you do not do something about solving the problems which cause the anxiety, it merely maintains the anxiety at a fairly high level which is damaging to the heart, lungs, and the cardio-vascular system. In practising relaxation, have two goals: Clear your body of anxiety so that you can return to a healthy resting state, thus enabling you to think clearly and solve problems, and second, having an "on the spot" technique which helps you relax and stay calm in difficult situations.

EXERCISES

Relaxation

During the day
Take time out during the day to relax and reflect on your day.

Mid-day Break 10 to 30 minutes
Find a place where you can be quiet and undisturbed. If that is difficult, sit in your car; if no other options are available, sit in the loo. You need time to shut off and to be undisturbed. Shut your eyes and go through the relaxation exercise or listen to the relaxation tape.

Early Evening 10 to 30 minutes
After the main work of the day is done, and you are in transition from one sphere of your life to another, take time to relax and wind down. Some people find that it is very helpful to clear their minds of the tasks of the day by reviewing the day's agenda and making notes of what needs to be done tomorrow. Don't keep it in your head — write it down and forget it.

If you are in a transition from work to home, take some time to relax your mind and get rid of your body's tension. If you are travelling by public transport, go through the RELAXATION EXERCISE. This is also a great way to cope with long plane journeys and avoid jet-lag.

If driving your car, turn your mind off from the day's work and problems by listening to a tape or the radio. If you find listening to music doesn't shut off your internal dialogue, turn to a radio station with talking — Quiz programmes are the best. When you have arrived at your destination, sit quietly in your car for about 10 minutes, relaxing and releasing the tension caused by the journey and the build up during the day.

If you are at home, take some time out at least once a day to sit down and switch off. Again the most advantageous time is just before you switch gears, moving from your work or personal life to your family life, i.e., before you pick up the children from school, or before your spouse arrives home. Twenty minutes of relaxation at this point gives you renewed energy and allows you to put the troubles of the day (if there were any) into perspective.

Relaxation Exercise
If you practise this exercise every day for seven days, you will find that after that all you will need to do is to take several deep breaths and you will instantly relax.

Before you begin, decide how long you want to be relaxed, and tell yourself to be fully awake and refreshed in _____ minutes, or at a specific time. If you are concerned that you may fall asleep and not wake up in time, then set an alarm, but usually you can count on your brain to do it.

Get yourself into a relaxed position, either lying down or sitting in a comfortable chair. If you do sit, make sure your head is well supported.

1. Shut your eyes and get comfortable. Take a deep breath, filling your lungs as full as possible — hold your breath for a few seconds — and then slowly exhale and relax.

2. Breath in — hold it, and as you slowly exhale, feel your body begin to relax.

3. Breath in — hold it, and as you exhale, slowly push all of the air out of your lungs and relax.

4. Breath deeply — hold it and as you slowly push all the air out of your lungs, feel your body becoming more and more relaxed.

5. Breath deeply filling your lungs—hold it and as you slowly exhale, feel your

body becoming completely relaxed.

Now as you relax and continue to breath deeply, let the focus of your awareness slide down your body to the tips of your toes. As you become aware of your toes, feel the warmth of the relaxation spread across your toes and spread up through your feet, up to your ankles. Feel your feet becoming warm, then numb and relaxed. The relaxation is now spreading up through your legs, up to your knees, and as it does, feel your legs becoming heavier and heavier and relaxed.

Relaxation is now spreading up across your knees, up through your thigh muscles, up to your hips, and as you breathe deeply and relax, feel your entire legs becoming numb and heavy and relaxed. Relaxation is now spreading upward, slowly upward, vertebrae by vertebrae up your backbone; up past your waist, up past your shoulder blades; up to your shoulders. Now feel your entire body becoming heavy, relaxed and pressed against the floor.

Breath deeply — hold it and feel your body becoming heavy, and relaxed as you exhale. As you continue to relax, become aware of the relaxation starting in your finger tips. As the relaxation starts there, feel your fingers becoming first warm, then tingly, then numb and relaxed. The relaxation is now spreading throughout your hands, gradually spreading upward across your wrists up through your arms, up to your elbows; gradually rising up through your upper arms, up to your shoulders. Feel your arms becoming warm, then numb, then heavy and relaxed.

As the relaxation spreads upward across your shoulders, feel your shoulders becoming light and free as the burdens you may carry there fall away one by one. Relaxation is spreading upward, through your neck, gradually rising up through your head, warmly spreading across the top of your head, down across your forehead. As you feel the relaxation spreading, feel your face becoming calm and peaceful and relaxed. Relaxation is spreading down around your eyes, moving slowly downward across your cheeks, down around your mouth. Feel your entire face becoming peaceful and calm and relaxed.

Breath deeply, and feel your entire body very relaxed and at peace.

In this relaxed state, let your mind drift, enjoying the leisure of not thinking or, if you wish, wandering back in time to an happy occasion in the past where the sun was warm, the sky was blue, and you felt calm, warm and relaxed. Stay there in this relaxed mode until you are ready to return to the present, fully awake, with renewed energy, calm and relaxed.

On the Spot Relaxation

There may be times when you need to instantly become calm and relaxed — times when you need to think well or when you are being criticized. In order to do this, it would help if you have practised the **RELAXATION EXERCISE** previously.

1. Take a deep breath and calm down.
2. Get into a relaxed position.
3. Take another deep breath and as you slowly exhale, feel the tension leaving your body, and your whole body relaxing while your mind remains clear and alert.
4. Repeat Step 3 two more times.

RELAX, BREATH, STAY CALM AND THINK.

CHAPTER 9
PROTECTION SKILLS II

How to Assertively Deal with Criticism

What is the number one fear we all have in dealing with people? It's being criticized, isn't it? For some of us, the anxiety and fear which is aroused by the anticipation of criticism is more dreadful than the actual criticism. Some of us behave as if we see others as people who have the power of life and death over us and act as if we have just been threatened with death when criticized. It is amazing how criticism can have such a powerful effect on people—or is it? Let's have a look at criticism to see what has happened to make it such a powerful weapon.

To do so, you need to journey back in time, to the time you were a child. As a very small child your existence in this world is a fairly precarious affair. For example, in the Western culture you need a human adult to look after you, provide you with the basic necessities such as food, shelter, clothing, and to keep you safe until you are eight years old, or you will die. Each baby coming into the world has the knowledge of its precariousness and of its dependency lodged somewhere deep inside it. As well as the dependency issue, there is also the vital need for recognition of existence by the baby's parents which is another crucial life and death issue. As seen in the studies of Rene Spitz,[17] if babies under the age of two years do not get this recognition, they will die, and this most vital recognition is, at that age, touching. As demonstrated so dramatically by Harry Harlow,[18] who raised monkeys with surrogate mothers, if touching does not occur—or other forms of recognition—little monkeys pathetically grow up schizophrenic. So too, do little human children. Children who are not touched, cuddled or fondled, or not touched appropriately enough to fill the need, or who do not perceive that recognition, can grow up emotionally at risk, and/or physically and/or mentally retarded. Hence the importance of the slogan, "Have you hugged a child today?" As the child grows older the physical recognition of touch, turns into verbal recognition. Verbal recognition comes in two forms: praise or criticism. The absence of recognition leads to a fairly serious position for the child. If the child is raised in a family where praise or positive recognition is scarce, they will learn to do things to get attention in other ways. They actually learn to seek negative attention because, "Bad strokes are better than no strokes".[16] How often can you remember only being told about the things you did that were bad or wrong, and not about the things you did that were good? In organizational parlance that is the philosophy of, "If you don't hear from us you will know you are doing OK", "Don't worry, we'll tell you when you are wrong." And worry you do, as if you have the Sword of Damacles hanging over your head. Without positive feedback to offset the "worry" you most certainly will trip up, do things to be criticized for.

With such a strong incentive to keep parents around and to keep parents as happy as possible, while trying to get recognition from them, the child learns to do what the parents want it to do at a fairly early age. Fear of withdrawal of recognition and disapproval are the strong negative motivators. The positive incentive to behave as parents want is approval, and the giving of positive recognition, which means to the child that it is safe and wanted, and in the ultimate, loved. If you will look at Figure 18 you will see how this is done:

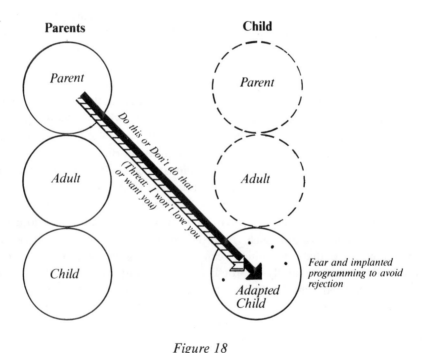

Figure 18
Learning Criticism

Because these programmes are put in with such strong emotional issues, it creates very sensitive spots in the Child which we call "Hurt Buttons". These buttons are extremely sensitive — like a burn or injury which has not healed and is super-sensitive to pain. So sensitive, in fact that it does not require the person who was originally responsible for the implanting of the buttons to now run the programmed-responses. It only requires that that person is similar in looks, voice tones, gestures, mannerisms, choice of words, and whoosh, the whole critical process is ignited—complete with all the old feelings of hurt, fear and rejection. When your buttons are pushed, you respond from your Adapted Child, and the same old records play the same old themes with the same old outcomes. Bad.

The Good News
The above is a process familiar to everyone at one time or another and in varying degrees of bad outcomes. We can use some of our common sense skills to change this. Desensitize our over-sensitive spots and, if you wish, turn criticism into a postive form of problem solving.

Do you remember the Three Laws of Communication we met in Chapter Two? Law Number One said, "If the Ego State which is targeted responds, and responds back to the Sending Ego States, a complementary transaction takes place and communication can continue indefinitely on that level." If we respond back from the Adapted Child with an old programmed response we are likely to maintain the Role Positions established; the other person being in the Superior Critical Parent or "I know best position" and you in the Inferior, "I'm not as good as you", Adapted Child position. Remember that the Adapted Child either complies (gives in) or rebels ("You're not so good"). So this is what we do not do when responding to criticism:

THE DO NOTS
DO NOT:
GIVE IN
ARGUE
COUNTERCRITICIZE
USE SARCASM
SAY NOTHING
JUSTIFY
BECOME DEFENSIVE

THE DO'S
That's what you do not do. What you do in it's place is use Communication Law

Number Two: "When the Ego State which was targeted doesn't respond, but another Ego State does, and responds back to a different Ego State, there is a "crossed transaction and communication ceases, at least on that level". Cross up that Parent to Child transaction by responding from Adult, staying unemotional and acknowledging the facts involved, or cross-up the critical transaction from Nurturing Parent with understanding or empathy. That perhaps sounds a little complicated, so try the common sense approach of, "Confuse them with facts", and "Surprise them with understanding."

As with the Presentation Skills there is a very simple 1-2-3 Step guide to help you put it into operation.

Dealing With Criticism

1. *Listen and Acknowledge:* the critic or the criticism.
2. *Define:* the problem.
3. *Solve:* the problem.

Putting it to Work

Step One
Step 1. *Listen and Acknowledge the critic or criticism or the problem.*
As in the 1-2-3 Steps to Assertive Requests, listening is the first and most important step. Be a good listener. Listen to what is said so you can get an accurate picture of the problems, and respond to what is specifically said, not what you think is meant, intended or hinted at. Don't mind-read, stick to the words as presented.

Acknowledging the critic can be as simple as saying "OK", or, "It sounds as if there is a problem", or simply repeating back in question form, what the critic has said to you, e.g., "Are you saying that you don't like the way I speak to you?", to the criticism of, "You can certainly tell one's upbringing when one talks to a person like that", and ignore the implications that you are some kind of inferior being.

Acknowledging the criticism sometimes looks like agreeing with it. What you are intending to demonstrate is that you are willing to listen, even to the things being said to you which may not be too favourable or pleasing to you. Why this is called a protection skill is that we are protecting ourselves, our self-esteem, or our sensitive spots, without becoming aggressive and counter-attacking, and without backing down. Our purpose here is to deflect or dilute the personal attack while hopefully giving the message that we will hear them out and look at what they're saying. Several ways to do that are to:

ACKNOWLEDGE THAT:

A: *Criticism is an opinion, and people can have differing opinions, but that opinions are not necessarily facts.*
You can use phrases as: "I can see your point of view." "That's one way of looking at it." "I can see why you think 'x,y,z' ", but note that you are not acknowledging that they are right.

B: *There is a possibility that they are right.*
You could say: "You *could* be right about that." "There is that possibility." "That's possibly true", but you are *not* saying they are *right*.

C: *There is always room for improvement, no one is perfect.*
You might say: "Yes, I could do that differently couldn't I?" "I'm sure there are a number of other ways I could approach that." That might be an interesting way to do it." Don't say, "I could have done it better". That implies that what you have done, you have done badly, and you are complying with the criticism.

D: *The part of the criticism that is true.*
If someone makes a sweeping statement that everything you have done to date is a mess, you might say: "Yes, the report I submitted was incorrect", or, "You are right, I haven't done as well as I could today have I?"

E: *Show understanding.*
Behind many criticisms there are upset feelings or a problem which needs to be resolved. You could empathetically put yourself in the other person's shoes and say, "I can see that this is causing you some distress or inconvenience", or, "I know how very disappointed I would be if that happened to me. If I arrived for a meeting after a long journey and found out it had been cancelled I would be very annoyed too. Would you like to use my phone?" Yes Madam, if I paid all that money for fancy knickers and had the elastic break on the first wearing I would be very unhappy with the product and the people who sold them to me. Let's have a look at them."

F: *Admit genuine errors.*
If you really have made a mistake or error, admit it in a straightforward manner, don't respond to any of the said or implied parts about you as a not-OK person. What you say, without fail is: "Yes, you are right." "Yes, I did make a mistake," "Yes, that is wrong."

'How to assertively deal with criticism; admit genuine errors.'

Create a fog

Manuel Smith, in *"When I say no I feel guilty"*,[11] thought of a good way of putting this deflecting into practice. He said to, "Think of yourself as a fog bank", and this technique is commonly called "fogging". Anyone can walk into a fog bank. That means you are approachable. "But have you ever had any success pushing a bank of fog, pulling one, squeezing one, twisting or turning one?" As with a bank of fog, you cannot be manipulated. "It also gives nothing hard to strike against." That says you simply absorb the aggressive energy from the other person. Since you give nothing back to fuel their aggression, they soon deplete their supply of anger and their aggressive attack fizzles out. Another way to use the fog bank is to think of it as a protective blanket of foam which covers your hurt buttons, and does not allow the aggressor to get through. It also puts a blanket of little droplets of water on the fire of the aggression and takes the heat out of the encounter. What you will find is that the critic either ceases the criticism or takes the "sting" out of the criticism, and like a balloon which has been pricked, loses its' hot air.

To do this, get yourself in a comfortable position, let the chair take the strain if you are sitting, or, if you are standing assume your Assertive Stance and find an object to give you a little support, like a chair, desk or counter top to put your hand on. Remember: BE A GOOD LISTENER. LISTEN WITH YOUR ADULT. LISTEN, DON'T FORMULATE ANSWERS INSTEAD OF

112

LISTENING. RESPOND TO WHAT IS SAID, NOT WHAT YOU THINK IS MEANT, OR MIGHT BE INTENDED. STAY IN YOUR ADULT.

Look at the person but dilute direct eye contact, sometimes that hard aggressive stare can be very intimidating. Look at the critic's nose, eyebrows, face. Look away to keep your comfort level, but do remember to come back and look at the person.

WATCH POINTS: *In a personal or working relationship, do not use a deflecting or diluting response more than twice in a row.*
If you have deflected twice and the critic comes back again, move on into problem solving—Step 2. This person is trying to tell you that there is a problem and there is nothing more frustrating than trying to solve a problem or explore feelings than to have it shrugged off by someone who continues to fog.

Second point to watch for: *Fogging tends to be fairly passive, and remember the Old Psychological Law:- Passivity escalates aggression in other people.*
Be active, make your responses as lengthy as possible instead of the constant flows of "You could be right" and "I hear what you are saying". Tell what they could be right about, and what it is that you are hearing.

EXERCISES

Developing a language for dealing with criticism
To be able to slip into your Assertive language while you are being criticized is difficult. You have to practise saying the phrases before hand, so that when you are "under fire", you can open your mouth and the right words come out.

Choose five phrases and practise them.

Caution: Learn at least five different phrases. If you stick to the same old one or two, you will drive people mad or make them angry with you.
Suggested deflecting or diluting phrases:
    I can see your point of view.
    I can understand why you think that.
    That's an interesting way of looking at things.
    That's an interesting idea.
    I hadn't thought of that.

What you are saying is _____
That's possible.
That could be so.
You might have a point there.
I haven't looked at it that way.
The part that _____, is right,.
Hum.
Interesting.
You could be right.

1.   Write down your five favourite phrases.

_____

_____

_____

_____

_____

2.   Memorise your five phrases so you can say them easily.
3.   When you can say them easily, practise nodding your head "yes" in
     the affirmative.

Practice by yourself

3.   Now think of the person or people you find it difficult to take
     criticism from.
     Picture that person.
     Picture looking them in the eye and imagine saying your fogging phrases
     and saying their name after each one.
     First practise on someone easy, i.e., a shop assistant, a child, or on some-
     one you don't know. When you have had some practice, try your phrases
     with people who are more difficult but again, start with the easy ones and
     build up to the more difficult people.

Practice with others

If you have someone who is particularly difficult, or a situation which is
difficult, practise outloud what you will say with a friend, before you go into
action.

Criticism: Step Two

New Lamps for Old: Turn Criticism into Problem Solving
Step Two: *Find out what the problem is. Ask for the facts.*

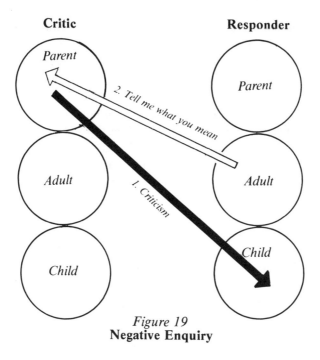

Critic   **Responder**

Parent

Parent

2. Tell me what you mean

Adult   *Adult*

1. Criticism

Child

Child

Figure 19
Negative Enquiry

Once again we have a Communication Law to help us. Communication Law
No. 3 says we can operate on more than one level at the same time. Once again
we will use it to our advantage to get the problem separated from the criticism. If
you look at the diagram in Figure 19, you will see that our object is to get the
other person to tell us what their Parent is annoyed or irritated about, not
demonstrate it as they were previously doing; or tell us what their Child is upset
with or aggrieved by, not demonstrate it as they were doing previously. If we are
successful in this manoeuvre, we can get the other person to use their Adult Ego
State to report on their Parent annoyances or report on their Child feelings.
Since Adult is unemotional, we should be able to have a reasonable discussion
and get to the heart of the problem without emotions and bad feelings getting in
the way of problem solving.

Here's how to. Again, we have Mr. Smith to thank for a handy technique. He
calls it "Negative Enquiry". This technique allows you to Assertively enquire
about information which may be negative about you. Here are some guiding
steps to Stage Two.
First: *Acknowledge that you have heard the critic, or dilute the critical intent.*
Second: *Find out what the problem is.* Specify the dynamics.
Third: *Summarize what you have heard.*
Fourth: *Ask if there is more.*

To accomplish Step 2, you need to ask specifying questions. Specifying questions are words which will get the person to respond with Adult information, stop generalising and name calling and tell you specifically what the problem is. The specifying questions are *Who, What, When, How, Where, How much, How many,* and *Which.* One of the specifying questions we do not use is *Why.* Why runs the risk of once again eliciting a Critical Parent opinion, and we've been working hard trying to stay in Adult ourselves and getting the other person to do likewise. That says we have to get Mr. Lips and Mr. Tongue to form new ways of getting "Why" information. Examples of these substitutes are, "*What* is the problem?" "*How* is it a problem?" "Can you give me an *example?*", instead of using "why".

Summarize
Once we have found out what the specific deeds or problems are which were couched in "all", "none", "everything", "always", "never", or have a definition of the annoyance or the upset, we *recap.* It shows the other person we really are listening, and it makes sure we have it right.

Exhaust the criticism
Finally, ask if there is something else they would like to tell us. This is for a number of reasons. First, people usually have a number of grievances — remember the stamp collection? — and only tell about one at a time. More important is the idea that they usually keep the most important one until bottom of the list. It is the one which usually bears the strongest feelings and is therefore potentially the most destructive. It seems reasonable to believe that that one really needs to be brought into the open and aired. If you don't and you allow the other person to harbour it, much of the previous problem solving will have been for nought.

WATCH POINTS: Notice, at no time have we said we caused the problem, or that we are a bad or a not-OK-person. Also, we have not become apologetic, believing that actions at this point are more important than apologies.

EXERCISES

Dealing with Criticism

Step 2
After you have acknowledged the critic or the criticism — or diluted the critical

attack — practise your enquiring phrases:

Opening the Enquiry

I'm not sure I understand, or,

I'm not quite clear, or,

There are some points I'd like to clarify,

or, think of your own opening phrases.

Defining the problem

Practise asking your *Specifying Questions* to get them to describe the problem.

> *Will* you tell me:
>
> *What* do you mean?
>
> *Which* one specifically?
>
> *When* did this happen?
>
> *Who* are you talking about?
>
> *Where* did this happen?
>
> *How* is that a problem?
>
> *How* is that wrong or bad?
>
> *What* don't you like about it?
>
> *What* is wrong with it?

Practise saying these outloud and add your own phrases.

Summarizing the information gained:

What you are saying is _____

So it's _____

that is wrong or bad or that you don't like?

Ask for the rest

Is that all or is there more?

Solution: Step 3

Step 3: *Find out what would solve the problem*

With the problem clearly defined, and the other person talking fairly factually about the problem, it is time to move to the solution phase. Here's the guide.

A. *Ask for a solution.* "What would solve the problem?", or "What would you like done about it?".

B. *Suggest or tell a solution* Get an OK!

If you ask the question about a solution and get a negative answer or a, "What do you think we pay you to do around here?". then state a solution. When you state a solution, always check with the other person that they have understood what you are suggesting and that you get an OK for that solution from the person. If you are concerned about the other person's memory, put the solution in writing and get a written OK. People who are critical by nature are like yoghurt makers. They keep something of this batch behind so they can start the next one. The story of a young buyer for a company comes to mind here. He, because of his inexperience in the job, misjudged a "chance of a lifetime" offer from a supplier. His manager was hardly subtle with his criticism when he confronted him with the dastardly deed. "We could have all retired and been on Easy Street if it hadn't been for your stupidity." The language is of course cleaned-up here to get past the the censors. "Should I go back and order more?" asked the younger buyer, "Of course, you jerk", came the reply. He did. He quadrupled the order. The next transaction from his superior was, apart from the names he called him, to fire him. "But you told me to order more." "Yes, but I didn't say that much more." Moral of the story: always be specific about what you propose to do and get a clear confirmation.

What about the situation where you may have said something which was misinterpreted by the other party, or inadvertantly hit on a sore spot? It may have been that a "spur of the moment" action has caused offence or upset. You can't re-do these situations because it has happened and it is over. What you can do is to *offer an apology, and/or to give an assurance* that you will be more sensitive to their feelings in the future, and/or that you will not behave in that way again.

WATCH POINTS: Notice that we have not agreed that we caused the problem or the error, nor have we actually made a commitment to enact the solution, and we certainly have not agreed with their definition of us as a bad or Not-OK person.

At this point, if the solution to the problem is acceptable to you, go ahead and agree to carry it out. If it is not, if the other person is way off in their analysis of the problem, then revert to the 1-2-3 Guide to Assertively state your position and offer your solution. If there is some truth in what they say, but you cannot accept the whole situation, then offer a compromise.

Dealing with Angry Criticism
There are those occasions when people get themselves so worked up with anger when giving criticism that sometimes whatever you say or do only serves to

make them angrier. What is suggested here is that you use STEP 1 to acknowledge on a very low level that you are paying attention and hear them, but that you do not attempt to move into problem solving at that time. Delay STEPS 2 and 3 until a later date, when the emotion has passed, and if possible, in private. After the heat of the event has died away, and you have done no damage, you can open the procedure with a simple, "I'd like to talk with you about this morning", for example. However, don't be too surprised if the barrage starts again. If so, once again refuse to discuss the problem unless the shouting and screaming stops. It may be appropriate at some time to tell the person at the later discussion that he or she is a bully, and to stop treating you like that. With some of these people, they continue to behave the way they do because no-one is straight and tells them the way it is.

People in this state are sometimes not only unable to be reasoned with, they are unwilling to be reasonable. They don't want to hear what you have to say, nor do they particularly want to solve problems. These are people who use anger and aggression to frighten or bully people into submission. Their philosophy is that the only management style which is effective is to be a bully. So stay calm, take a deep breath, listen and acknowledge.

EXERCISES

Stage 3 Solving the Problem
1. *Ask*
"What would you like me to do?" or,
"What would solve the problem?"
Repeat back: OK, so if I were to (solution) _____
_____

that would solve the problem?
or

2. *Tell*: This is what I can do (solution) _____
_____

2b. *Get an acknowledgement*: "Is that OK?" (yes or no).
If *No*, go back to *Ask*.

Taking care of hurt feelings or past "personal injustices".
Ask: What would help?

or

Offer an apology: I'm sorry your feelings are hurt.
I'm sorry you feel that way.

and,

Give assurance: I will give you my assurance that I won't do that again.

Criticism which you disagree with:

A: *Say Deflecting or Diluting Phrases.* See page 113.

B: *Then use Sliding Phrases*: Practise the following sentences until you can say four very easily and naturally.

On the other hand, _____

On the same hand, _____

If you look at it this way, _____

However, _____

In a different vein, _____

In the same vein, _____

Looked at from this angle, _____

However, from my point of view, _____

C: *End with an Assertive Statement:*
Finish each statement with your facts.

This is what I think, _____

_____

This is how I see it, _____

_____

My reasons are, _____

_____

This is what happened _____

_____

These are the facts as I see them, _____

_____

Criticism which is true:

Assertive Phrase: "Yes, you are right about (and state the fact — ignoring the personal put-down). _____

_____

CHAPTER 10
GIVING CRITICISM

Now that you are fully aware of what it is like to be on the receiving end of bad criticism, and how hard you have to work to turn it into something positive, let's look at giving criticism in a constructive way. You will have to give criticism from time to time in your life. You may have the responsibility of correcting people when they make mistakes or do things which are inappropriate to the situation. If you are in charge of people either at work or in a social context, it makes good sense to point out situations and give advice, where there are more appropriate forms of action. If you are a parent, or responsible for parenting children in some way, you not only have the responsiblility to see to it that their behaviour is corrected, or that they are shown more appropriate ways of behaving, but it is an essential act of love. It says you care enough about the child or the person to see to it that they know how to live and behave in an effective way. When you are involved in personal relationships with people, it is productive for you and for the relationship to point out things people do or say which are harmful to the friendship or hurt you personally. How many times have friendships drifted apart because one person has taken offence at the words or actions of the others, but had failed to say anything or do anything. Probably the biggest cause for marriages to break up is that the partners don't know how to tell each other in a constructive way about things they would like the other to change or stop doing. What is more common is for criticism to be given in a hostile or sarcastic manner. Another favourite way is to sit on it, "collect stamps", until you can't contain it any more and then let fly with the lot thus cashing in your stamps. The result is that almost miraculously there is total recall for every past misdeed, digging them all up and hurling them all at the offending party. In the heat of the moment, much is said from that pea-sized brain which is usually regretted later, and calls for apologies or trying to make amends if the person is still around. Wouldn't it be better to be able to come out with the criticism at the time and in an amount which is appropriate to the deed, in a manner which avoids or eliminates the destructive elements.

The same phenomena occur in the work environment. Management avoids giving the "bad news", preferring to keep secret "hit lists" which are used to justify no promotion or lack of salary increases, rather than give people information about their performance or personal habits which need changing. They lie to the person, sometimes by omission, preferring to push the person aside, keeping them on as "dead wood", and shedding them when they have no other choice. This is usually in times of economic recession, when the person in question has little opportunity to move to new employment because of age or scarcity of jobs. How much better to give people the opportunity to change or reorganize their lives or the way they do things, rather than shying away from the "embarassing task". Most organizations have recognized this and implemented a system of periodic reviews called performance appraisals. Even if your organization does not have a formal appraisal system, there is nothing to stop you from initiating your own. Now that you are assertive and can ask for things and take criticism, ask your boss to go through your job and tell you not only what you could change or improve on, but what you are doing well and he or she is pleased with. Ask for the praise as well as the criticism.

Performance appraisals are like any other system — only as good as the people who operate them. When used effectively they are a review or crystallization of the on-going praise and criticism the subordinate gets on a daily basis. There is a rule of thumb to follow here. A performance review should contain no surprises either to the subordinate or the boss. You stand the best chance of getting the best out of people if you tell them what is wrong when the event occurs. People actually learn quicker with less negative feelings when critical information is given as close to the event as possible. Memory has a strange way of distorting sequences and events and people do forget. So don't hang around. Give criticism early — but give praise early as well.

One other point to remember, because some criticism is embarassing or distasteful to us, we sometimes become very awkward in describing the problem. This is particularly true if it is criticism of the person's more personal habits, like personal hygiene or social habits. If you don't come to the point quickly enough, you may scare them into believing that there is something far more serious happening. There is the story about the female mananger who had the task of telling one of her subordinates that she had B.O. and asking her to do something about it. She beat around the bush so much, using "nice" but inaccurate descriptions of the problem, such as "a personal problem of a social nature", that when the girl finally found out that all she had was B.O. she started to cry. "Oh", she said, "You had worried me so. I was beginning to think I was about to be arrested or fired for some terrible deed that I had done, or that I was some kind of freak." If the person has some annoying habits, tell them what they are. Be kind but be direct.

Here's the guide to help you give constructive criticism.

Giving Criticism
1. Establish communication with the other person.
2. State the problem. Be specific and direct.
3. Ask for a solution. Get a commitment for action.

When you know you have to criticise someone, don't just approach the subject cold. Have some conversation first. However, don't feign interest in the person just because you have some bad news to tell. Don't ask questions and then not listen to the answer, like the manager who had to criticise a sales person and opened the conversation by asking her how she and her children were. "Not too good", came the response. "I have just learned that my youngest daughter has leukemia." "Fine", said the supervisor, "Glad to hear it", and then moved on to give his criticism. Not only was he not listening, but he was not responding on a sensitive level at all as to the appropriateness of the timing of his criticism.

If you can say something positive about the person or relationship—*and mean it*—then do so. If you have to invent something, then it sounds patronising and false, it will be received negatively and the person will not trust you. Also, if you do not say positive things about them, their work, etc., on an on-going basis, *do not do so only when giving criticism*. That sets up the situation of "first the good news, then the bad news", and they will not hear or believe the good things you have said. It builds distrust.

We have already covered the reasons for being clear and coming straight to the point. Asking for a solution is different from telling a solution. If you ask the person to come up with a solution, you are giving responsibility to the person for solving the problem. You are, in effect saying to them, "Come on you can do it. You can think and solve problems". There is a higher probability that the person will actually solve the problem if *they* decide how to do so. You are saying, "This is what I want the outcome to be." "How you go about it is up to you." If you tell the other person how to do it, you could easily get involved in the game of "Why don't you?"—"Yes, but.." After you have listened to them, and heard reasons about why they can't, if you decide that it is still high on your priority list to set them to do as you have asked, or that they are giving you excuses and not real reasons, you can avoid a hassle by using Broken Record and insist on a solution. This works equally well with subordinates at work and particularly well with teenage children who love to hassle. If, on the other hand there are real reasons, you can offer to help in problem solving and/or negotiate a compromise.

EXERCISES

First, before you do anything, think about what you want to accomplish. What do you want this person to do differently:

Behavioural Objective
I want (person's name) to do: _____

_____

_____

_____

_____

Step One: Open the Conversation.
If you can, say something positive about the person — but only if you mean it and it doesn't sound patronising. *Listen* to what the person says to you and then decide:

    a. Is this the time and the place?

    b. Is the situation as I had assessed it?

If the answers are *YES* then move to Step 2.
If the answers are *NO*, then do a re-think or choose another time or place.

Step Two: State the Problem.
Be tactful, but don't beat around the bush. State what the problem is or how it is a problem for you.
THIS IS THE PROBLEM: _____

_____

_____

_____

_____

Step Three: State a solution or ask for a solution.
Get a commitment. Stay with it until you get it. If the person says they will try, show your appreciation for their efforts, but persist until you have a commitment that they will *do it*.
You may also wish to set a time target by which you want the objective achieved.
SOLUTION: _____

_____

_____

_____

TIME TARGET: _____

CHAPTER 11
FEELINGS

We've made much of staying in Adult, being in control and unemotional. If it were the case that feelings were not important and only Adult reasoning and logic were necessary to be effective we would find being effective very easy, and effective behaviour would be very easy to acquire. However, this is not the case. Only by making some major adjustments in your personality could you suppress or cut off your feelings. If you did so, you would become robot-like, boring and tedious. You may know someone who made this kind of adjustment. People regard them as dry, lacking a sense of humour, and not very stimulating to live with or work with. Since it is inadvisable for anyone to make adjustments of this nature, let's have a look at feelings and how to express them appropriately, for it is feelings which give spice and excitement to your personality and lives.

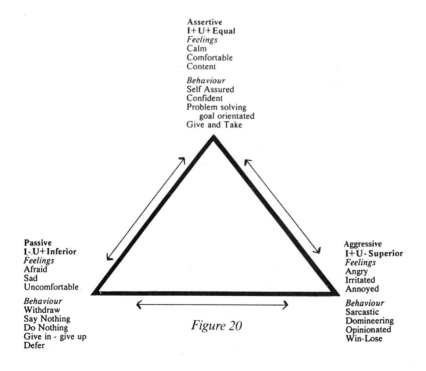

Assertive
I+U+Equal
Feelings
Calm
Comfortable
Content

Behaviour
Self Assured
Confident
Problem solving
    goal orientated
Give and Take

Passive
I-.U+Inferior
Feelings
Afraid
Sad
Uncomfortable

Behaviour
Withdraw
Say Nothing
Do Nothing
Give in - give up
Defer

Aggressive
I+U- Superior
Feelings
Angry
Irritated
Annoyed

Behaviour
Sarcastic
Domineering
Opinionated
Win-Lose

Figure 20

125

Natural Feelings/Learned Feelings

As you will recall from an earlier chapter, feelings and feeling behaviour are, in the beginning, nature's way of getting your basic needs met, both physical needs and emotional needs. There are three primary natural feelings: *anger, fear,* and *contentment*.

If you will refer to the behaviour triangle in Figure 20, you will see that they correspond to the three behavioural positions.

Sadness, which is found in Passive Behaviour, although a natural feeling is not a *primary* feeling because an experience of loss or withdrawal of a loved object or person is necessary in order for this feeling mechanism to become operative. Sadness is sometimes thought of as a mixture of the two feelings, of anger and fear. Fear, because of the precarious nature of being left or deserted, and the anger at the loss. This anger is usually turned inward. Natural feelings are those feelings which we express with only small alterations to the original feeling process. For example: Danger stimulates *fear*. Encroachment on, or threat to, territory, family or self, leads to *anger. Loss* of a loved one, or hopes and dreams, or a loved object, brings on *sadness*. Love, attention, self-satisfaction, excitement, create happy or content feelings. However, as we grow up, we learn that there are certain feelings which should not be expressed for reasons which are specific to our families or cultures, and there are feelings which we learn to give precedence to over others. We also learn to express our feelings in certain ways. These are called "preferred" feelings, and every family and every culture has its favourites.

Cultural Bias

As well as the family bias for preferred feelings, our culture as we have seen, also enforces preferred feeling modes for women and for men. To complement the strong, aggressive male script, men learn to *Be Strong* which means, don't cry, don't show fear, don't show pain or hurt, either emotional or physical. In order to subdue or suppress those feelings of pain, fear or vulnerability, the soft feeling of love, closeness, and tenderness have to be subdued as well for the same emotional mechanisms in each process are involved. Men are given a double incentive to adopt this feeling pattern. Recognition is given to the strong, fearless man—while men who show the feelings are labelled as "wet" and "cissy".

Men then learn to express "hard" feelings as their feelings release mechanisms which displace the more natural feeling of pain, fear, tenderness or vulnerability. Since anger is the more available feeling, it is the most prominent feeling in the male repertoire and the easiest to access. Closeness involves vulnerability, and often to protect this vulnerability, anger is escalated over the fear and is either expressed directly or indirectly. The resulting patterns of behaviour are provocative, critical or angry which sets up a fight. This allows the person to find something to be angry about, or provokes someone else to be angry, so that the original anger is then justified. One might consider the provocative, angry, aggressive behaviour of young—usually male—delinquents, where in their homes and society, anger and toughness are the only feelings known and expressed. It is not only displacing love, but being angry which protects their vulnerability. It is common for them to respond to love and kindness with increased anger and aggression, because good feelings and acts often make them feel more vulnerable.

Women, on the other hand, are taught not to be angry, or not to show anger. It does not fit the classic conditioning of the nice, polite, pleasing, Passive Woman to be angry. As young girls, females are taught to be tired instead of angry, being sent to bed if they give a display of angry feelings, or told to hold their tongues and "Be Quiet". When, as adults, the conditioned feeling patterns are set, women are called names like, "shrew" or "bitch" if they display anger. More commonly, they are labelled "emotional" which is meant as a derogatory label because they have learned to cry from the frustration of the pressure of the anger build up, knowing they mustn't show it. They have learned then to displace angry feeling with sad feeling. They quietly hold their tongues, feeling sad with their helplessness, turning the anger inward, making the woman feel hopeless as well as helpless because they are now angry with themselves for being in that situation. Anger turned inward is a definition of depression, a condition experienced by many people, but more so by women rather than men.

Family Feeling Patterns
Put the two together, the denied feelings and the preferred feelings, and we have families who can be typed by their preferred feeling systems.

Quiet Family: is a quiet family. *Anger* is *not* acceptable. People walk around with a smile (often forced) and always looking for "the sunny side", while sometimes bristling with unexpressed anger or discontent underneath. They pretend everything in the garden is rosy, whilst they collect their anger stamps or divert anger into hypocrisy.

Family Gloom: has learned to be *sad*, "Oh I don't know, what's the point?", is their favourite family phrase. If someone is happy or had a happy event, they soon prick the bubble of the happy occasion by finding a flaw in the happiness. They have learned not to express happiness because something bad always follows something good. They often go around "bearing up".

Family Angry-Loud: are *angry*, critical and sarcastic. Whatever the occasion, the air is rife with attack and counter-attack. What is not accomplished by the more subtle forms of personal attack and sarcasm, is finished off with more bristling angry exchanges. Sometimes the loud volume of shouting and yelling is the order of the day. As one person put it, "I didn't know what ordinary talking was until I went to school. I thought everyone yelled all the time as they did in our family."

Doom Family: are waiting around for the unkown monster to jump out from behind the bushes to gobble them up. *Fear* is their No. 1 feeling. They are overly cautious, carefully monitoring their every move: "You can't be too careful", is their family motto. These are often the victims of the world, for their self-fulfilling prophecy is to have things happen to them; they have "bad luck".

Angry-Suspicious Family: are the families of suspicion and fear who counter their *fears* with *anger*. They use the message that "offence is the best form of defence". They sometimes take a disliking to others for no apparent reason. We are all like this at some time, but these more than others. They project their thoughts and motivations on to others, and then act as if it were true. The feelings here range from fearful suspicious to angry-attack.

Natural v Learned
When a natural spontaneous response follows a stimulus or event, we say that natural feelings are expressed. As we have seen, spontaneous feelings get changed because of family or cultural learning. Sometimes the changes are so extreme that we say a natural, spontaneous feeling has been displaced by a learned response or learned feeling. We call this kind of feeling a "displacement feeling".

How do we know the difference then, "Feelings are feelings". True. The displacement variety are feelings by any definition of feelings. You really do feel. There are however, some tests which can enable us to distinguish between displacement feelings and real feelings.

Displacement feelings:
A. Don't look right to an observer.
B. Linger on.
C. Don't quite fit the bill.

D. Don't satisfy the need; i.e., closure is not obtained and up they pop again.

Real or appropriate feelings:
Look right, feel right, and finish the job.

Expressing Feelings in the Natural Way

Undoing the Blocks to Spontaneous Feelings

As we have seen, some of the blocks to expressing feelings are there because of family or cultural taboos or traditions. Regaining your full complement of feelings is your aim. That encompasses all the feelings *anger, fear, sadness, happiness*. Part of the rediscovery process for you, then, is to learn to use your natural feelings in the way nature intended you to use them. To take care of yourself both emotionally and physically and enrich your relationships with people by using all your feelings.

There are a number of very good reasons why we *should* learn to do this. First relationships grow, becoming more rich and rewarding. Often to avoid natural feelings, or to produce the old, unfulfilling "displacement feelings", we play games with people we work with and live with, and end up with the bad feelings of anger, sadness and self-righteousness. Think of the rich rewards of "real feeling" relationships: fun, love and excitement. It is the difference between living life in black and white (sad, fear, despair), or red and white (anger, aggression), or technicolour—with all the colours of the rainbow—happy, sad, close, fun, anger and sorrow.

A second, and the major reason to learn to give up old feeling habits and learn new, is that the old patterns are emotionally and physically unhealthy for you: emotionally because they prescribe a general mind-set and life style which leads to mental unhealth—depression, suicide, psychosomatic illnesses, neurosis and even psychosis; physically because they damage your body. Living in an angry state, or on the verge of anger, causes the body to gear itself up for fight. The heart beats faster and harder, blood pressure increases, blood vessels constrict. The same thing happens with fear—the body gears itself up for flight or, if anger escalates over the fear, to fight. Both feeling responses initiate physiological changes in the body which simply wear it out earlier than normal. These, in our modern terminology, are called "Stress-related diseases". It is thought that certain forms of cancer, e.g., lung cancer, are related to these over-used feelings.

In the same vein, when anger is felt and not expressed, the body makes the necessary changes to be angry, but it is not allowed to express it, and the body does not return to a resting state. This perhaps is even more damaging because it prolongs the "at the ready" state. Other feelings — the displacement *expression* feelings of sadness, depression, etc., do help the body feel some kind of release from the "geared for action state", but since they do not solve the problem it is likely to occur, causing the body to once more "initiate" the wearing out behaviours. Once again, stress diseases are related to these displacement feeling states. Cancer of the breast and ulcers, are more common in women who suppress anger, ulcers, and stomach and duodenal cancers, for men and women who experience sadness or upset but do not express it.

'Regaining the full complement of feelings...anger, fear sadness, happiness.'

Expressing Natural Sadness, Pain, Hurt

When you are hurt or upset, what stops you from showing how you feel? Usually the thought of how you will look to others, even to the point of someone stepping on you — either literally or figuratively. You smile sweetly, bite your lip, because if you react, you fear you might go over the top. The natural reaction would be that if someone steps on your toes, you'd yell, "Ouch that hurts, don't do that". The same with emotional pain or hurt. If someone hurts you, the natural reaction would be to go ahead and express the pain or hurt. However, if

130

it is coupled with a thinking objective, i.e. how to prevent the person from repeating the act, you will lessen the number of times you will find yourself in that situation. You will find also that by adding a preventative act on to expressing your feelings, you won't feel as strongly at the time and the expression of feelings will be more acceptable to yourself as well as the others.

Here are some examples of preventative thinking or protective actions which are called Active Stoppers:

> *Active Stoppers*
> Don't.
> Don't do that.
> Stop that.
> That hurt.
> I didn't like that.
> Don't talk to me like that.
> That upsets me, don't.
> That hurts me, don't.

Said with feeling, they not only give the power of protection, but express the feelings of hurt, pain, or sadness.

Tears

The most controversial form of expression — next to anger — is tears. Some people, more commonly women, resort to them as a substitute for anger, and as frustration for not being able to be angry. They have the powerful effect of making others feel guilty, which probably is the reason why they are considered so undesirable. When looked at realistically, however, what is so terrible about tears? They have a very beneficial function. They relieve pressure and congestion which builds up in the upper chest, head and sinuses. The tear fluid washes the eyes, and this washing is, after all, the original meaning of catharsis. However, too many tears cause puffy eyes, red noses and become very tiresome for others who have to be around them.

When tears are appropriate. Tears are a great catharsis. When you are feeling sad, it is particularly difficult to think well. When something or someone has really upset you, go ahead and cry. It will make you feel better; it discharges the body/ brain system, and helps you think and act more effectively. There is nothing wrong with tears. That goes for men as well as women. Why is it unmanly for a man to demonstrate that he has feelings of pain, distress or hurt? These feelings are part of being human. How moving it is to see a great man demonstrate his qualities of humanity and caring by shedding a tear or two when moved by a touching occasion — and not ashamed to cry openly. As discussed in Chapter

One, one of the largest contributors to stress and stress disease is men suppressing their feelings. Moral of the story for men — more tears, less stress, live longer.

For women, the opposite is true. Because of their Passive scripting, they have not only used tears as a substitute for anger, but they have also taken on the feelings and tear-shedding for their non-feeling male counter-parts. At times in the work environment, tears are not necessarily conducive to being taken seriously. Instead of Passive tears or saying nothing, try the actions encouraged by Assertive behaviours, or expressing anger as demonstrated on page 134. You will find that the need for tears will diminish. If you find your feelings hurt easily, use the protective skills in Chapter 10. However, if you have done all these, and still feel sad or upset, go to the ladies room or somewhere private and cry. Cleanse your body and brain, and then *think* about what you need to do to prevent a recurrence of the situation. *Cry* in private; *think* to solve the problem; and *act* to deal with the situation.

Fear
Fear produces anxiety. A little anxiety adds zest to life. As we have seen before, anxiety is a motivator which prods you into action, and puts some feelings into your performance. However, too much fear or anxiety either in quantity or over a long period of time, incapacitates or causes behaviour adaptions. Either the person takes an avoidance pattern of behaviour, adopting passive patterns, or takes provocative actions, sometimes goading others into an angry or critical reaction to justify the internal feelings of fear. The third learned position is to escalate anger to fear to scare away the objects of fear. This depends on how real the perceived fear is. Sometimes we all over-react to people or a situation, perceiving danger where there is none, or not to the extent imagined. This justifies the internal, learned fear system.

Fear on the natural level is a healthy emotion. It tells us what to avoid that could cause harm, injury or hurt. However, the continuing feeling of fear is not healthy. The experience of fear which creates a healthy respect or adds a challenge to life is enough to experience excitement, other than that, thinking and protective actions are the order of the day. These are some guidelines to be able to separate out real danger from "learned or protective behaviour".

Think: a. Am I in danger?

b. Physical or emotional?

c. Is this real?

d. Should I run or fight or can I deal with this?

e. Use an Active Stopper, one internal, one external.

f. Give yourself encouragement to cope.

g. Counter the paranoid fantasy with, "it is not realistic to believe that people wish to do me harm. They are operating from their own motivation."

Anger

Our learning about anger is that we either over use it or under use it. Not many have an in between.

Over Use: The over use of anger is an ineffective operating system which maintains the win/lose positions, and makes personal and work relationships difficult if not impossible. Ever tried getting close to a hedgehog? Anger endangers long term goals, although it is quite effective in achieving short term gains; but gain by threat institutes a "management by fear" system, which is ultimately destructive.

Under Use: Some of us avoid anger for two reasons. We have been taught that being angry is not OK, or not an acceptable way to behave. Secondly, we may have seen aggression and anger modelled in our families in such a Not-OK way, that we decided that that was no way to behave. Some of us have the lurking suspicion that if we get angry, we will lose control and become irrational or unreasonably angry or violent. Unfortunately, the self-fulfilling prophecy works here. If we hold on to anger, attempting to sit on it, bite our tongues, etc., it does erupt sooner or later in the volcanic reactions of the over-the-mark anger.

Natural Anger: is a healthy, protective feeling. It is meant to frighten people or situations away who would do us harm. It allows us to clear the air, and lets the other person know precisely what's going on with us.

Controlled Anger

Can you be angry and in control? The answer is yes — more than you thought you could. It does not have to be all or nothing, you can be angry in varying degrees. Here's how:

Step One: Think of the outcome

What do you want to have happen? If a relationship, either working or personal, is involved, then go to Step 2; if not, or you don't care about the relationship, then simply express your angry feelings.

Step Two: Take care of the relationship and be angry

Say what the relationship means to you and then say what you are angry about while being angry. Be specific about the behaviour involved. Don't call the person names. For example, "I find working with you is usually productive and rewarding, but I'm very angry with you for going to the boss without telling me first. You really dropped me in it."

Step Three: Future actions
Say how you want them to behave in the future. For example. "I want you to tell me you won't do that again."

Anger to Stop Undesirable Behaviours
Sometimes, people especially if they are in an emotional state, are so involved with listening to themselves, staying with their own preceptions and not listening to you, that only by using a strong stopper, such as shouting or banging the table, will get them to stop and get their attention. Don't over use this or it will lose its' effectiveness. Save it for the very rare "once in a life-time" occasions.

Stopping Tears when Angry
Women who cry when angry, repeat the same act over and over with the same bad outcome: crying angry tears then fleeing from the room with embarrassment at their tears of frustration making their situation worse. Next time, stick it through. Whatever you do, *don't leave*, or if it is appropriate, *don't stifle your anger*, simply because you are afraid you might cry. Be angry and see it through, regardless of the tears. What are you ashamed of? So you are crying. Big deal. Go ahead, cry and be angry. What you will find happening is, that after a few times or maybe only one of being angry, and crying, but sticking to it, the tears will stop and you will be able to be angry without crying.

Contentment and Happiness
Being happy, and the ultimate of being happy, being in love, are often the most precarious states of being. There are people around who seem to enjoy stepping on happiness and happy feelings — the grumps of the world, who stomp around with expressions of "Get that grin off your face". "Stop that whistling". "No one should be smiling or laughing in this office or house on a Monday morning". Happiness is a feeling in the Child of delight, pleasure and contentment. Happiness, like all natural feelings, is derived internally. It may be stimulated by external events, but it is primarily the feeling generated from satisfaction in yourself first, and others second. Pseudo-happiness can be gained at the expense of others by rejoicing secretly or openly in their mistakes or misfortunes. How much of our so-called "humour" is misfortune-based? It could well be that this very warped idea of happiness has led to the uncaring and violence we experience in our modern society, where pleasure is gained

from others' misfortunes.

Love, being close, caring, are the strongest of the positive feelings, and like the negative feelings, are strong because they involve the greatest risk. No risk—no gain. Perhaps the most vulnerable position of all is to express your deep Child feelings to another person because it is the purest state of defencelessness and vulnerability. Love is unconditional. Since love is internally generated and is an expression of that internal state, it is not dependent on the other person performing in specified ways nor living up to your expectations. Love is because they are who they are, and you are who you are and feel what you feel.

Being Happy and Caring
If you have been an unhappy, or uncaring person, you have probably surrounded yourself with people who support that position, because people attract each other to fit their own behavioural styles. If you do wish to have full and caring relationships with others, as well as finding the happiness which life holds, you will need to be happy, have fun, be able to like and love. There are some suggestions at the end of the chapter which will help start down the yellow brick road. However, there are some cautionary notes. Because there may be these people currently in your life who enjoy acting like the big foot which appears from the sky to squash happiness, take care what you show to them or tell them. Maybe this is a time to do some sorting out and move away from those people who squash happiness.

Second, watch out for your "old self": that critical, self-censoring part that is left over from your past, responsible for your being unhappy today. Watch out for the vengence of the Old Critical Parent that squashes the delight of the Free child. Here is a place for some *internal* messages and encouragement for happiness. Say them to yourself.
Internal Encourager:

> It's OK to be happy.
> I'm OK.
> Being happy is Nature's Way.
> Happy is *NOT BAD*. It's good.
> I'm good.
> I deserve it!
> Good for me.
> Hurrah!
> Yippee!

The other thing to protect against is going overboard. Sometimes the way we get ourselves into trouble and misery is going over the mark — becoming the "life and soul of the party"; drinking too much and doing "crazy fun" things; becoming manic. To guard against these, plan the amounts of happiness, or pleasure you want and need, i.e., don't let yourself get too high. You must have some or you will go over the mark — because everyone has to have some enjoyment. Go through the exercises at the end of this chapter to regain your Natural Child feeling of happiness and contentment.

Smiling and Laughing

How do you show to yourself and others that you are happy? Usually by smiling or laughing. The stoppers here are again going overboard, either in what you think or what you do. Sometimes you think smiling means smiling all of the time, or a smile is a large, stupid grin on your face. That is not the case. You smile when it is appropriate, i.e., when you are pleased or delighted with yourself, someone else or something else. Smiling goes in degrees. A slight upturn of the corners of the mouth is a comfortable resting position which shows contentment and well-being. It is also a *comfortable* position for your face to assume. When you are really happy, pleased or delighted, open your mouth and really smile. Practice in front of a mirror for five minutes each morning. Formulas for rearranging your face into a pleased one without plastic surgery are found at the back of this chapter. Try them, you'll like them.

Laughing is another expression of well-being and happiness. Not, however, the undesirable laugh which comes from amusement or delight at others' misfortunes, but from happiness within you; what you like, or what delights you. Again, it is internal. Laughing is as cathartic as tears, yet with a better outcome for it has no lingering bad feelings. Laughing aids digestion, the communication process, and cements deeper and lasting relationships.

Some of us don't laugh because we have learned to be solemn and serious. Others of us avoid laughing because we have a laugh which is different from others, or perhaps we have been teased about laughing. As with tears, what does it matter? Your laugh is your laugh. So it's different, so what? What a monotonous world it would be if we were all the same and that includes laughing the same. You probably have an adapted laugh because you were stopped from enjoying and laughing naturally as a child. Anyway, who is it that sets the International Standards for Laughing, and in which Hall of Laughing are these standards kept?

Building up Your Feelings

Look at the exercises at the end of this chapter. Practise them until you have

136

your full complement of feelings, Anger, Sad, Fear and Happiness. When you have practiced them and built up your ability to express these spontaneously, appropriately and with comfort, you will be well on your way to being a very whole, together person. You can think and you can feel, just the way you could when you were little and using all of your natural equipment in the manner Mother Nature intended.

EXERCISES

Exercising Feelings

Sad
When I feel sad I _____

_____

It would be more appropriate to _____

_____

The last time I felt sad was _____

I should feel sad about (sad things which have occurred in your life)

_____

The last time I cried was _____
Losses I should cry about are _____

Angry
When I feel angry I _____

_____

It would be more appropriate to _____

_____

The last time I felt angry was when _____

_____

Situations I should be angry in are _____

_____

People I should be angry with are _____

_____

The next time (name of person) _____ says

_____

or does _____ I will show I'm angry by _____

_____

Fear

Phrases to use with people who frighten you:

"Stop that."
"Don't do that."
"I don't like that."
"Stop."
"Don't talk to me like that."
"That hurts me, stop that."
"That frightens me, stop that."
"Go away."

Practise saying each phrase 5 times. First just reading through, then with expression, then aimed at a person who frightens you.

Phrases to use in situations which frighten you

"I don't like this."
"I'm leaving."
"I have something else to do, I'm leaving."

Practise as above.

Actions to use when afraid

Change the subject.
Find someone else.
Leave.
Avoid the person.
Avoid the situation.

When I am afraid I usually _____

_____

It would be more appropriate if I _____

_____

The people I am afraid of are: _____

_____

Situations I feel afraid in are: _____

_____

Next time (person) _____ frightens me,

I will say (phrase) _____

_____

and do _____

Repeat out loud three times.

Happy

When I am happy, I show it by _____

_____

It would be more appropriate if I _____

_____

The last time I laughed was _____

_____

The things I like to laugh about are _____

_____

Repeat out loud three times.

Liking, Loving, Smiling

When I like someone I _____

_____

It would be more appropriate if I _____

_____

These are the people I like _____

_____

The next time I am with _____
whom I like, I will _____

_____

Loving

When I feel love for someone I usually _____

_____

I would be more appropriate if I _____

_____

The people in my life I love are _____

_____

The people in my life who love me are _____

_____

They show me they love me by _____

_____

How I would like them to show they love me is _____

_____

When I am with _____ whom I love,
I can show how I feel about them by _____

_____

_____

Liking

Start slowly. First of all keep it to yourself. Start in the morning by saying out loud:

Two things *I like:*
    1. That made me smile.
    2. About me.

Two things :
    1. I like about someone else.
    2. About someone else that make me smile.

Two things that:
    1. I like about life.
    2. That make me smile about life.

Evening
Two things that *I liked about today:*
    1. That made me smile today.
    2. I liked about life today.

If you can't find two then say one, but find something no matter how small.

Next step: Tell another person
One thing you like about them, and when you are braver, one thing about them that makes you smile.

When you are sure of that other person: Tell them,
One thing you like about life.
One thing you like about you.
One thing that makes you smile.

Smiling
1.   Look in the mirror and smile.
2.   Repeat several times until you are satisfied. When you are pleased with your smile, nod your head and think "that's good" as you smile.
3.   Now shut your eyes and remember what the smile looked like. Sometimes it helps to look upward as you do so.
4.   With your eyes shut, picture in your mind's eye what your smile looks like; form it, and then open your eyes to see how close you are to your mental

picture. Continue until you can form it with ease.

5.   Then every morning and as often as you can throughout the day, practise "smiling at the world", and watch the world smile back at you.

Laughing

Get yourself a tape recorder, and a book of funny stories or a joke book. Read the story or joke out loud into the tape recorder, and listen to your laugh.

A natural laugh, starts with a smile, and progresses from a chuckle to a good laugh as you open your mouth and throw your head back. Practise it. Remember something that was very funny and laugh about it. Like the other skills, it takes practice, as well as encouragement from you that it is OK to laugh and enjoy yourself.

FINISH

We've now come to the concluding phase of the first instalment. Like the continuing saga of the seven-year cycles of development, this is not the finale, only the end of the first wave of development/re-development. You are learning many things; knowing yourself and liking yourself. Showing you can think, feel, be decisive and in control. You are also learning how to ease your life around difficult people. Perhaps most important of all, you're getting some controlled feelings into your life which should make your life more exciting and fun as well as worthwhile and powerful. Now it's time to start the next phase.

At the beginning, you set yourself some objectives. Go back and have a look at them. How well have you done? If you have not accomplished everything you intended to, say, "Well done" for *anything* you have accomplished, and reward yourself. Rate yourself on a scale 1-10 and you will see you have accomplished something. If there is more to do, start the next phase by setting yourself three new targets. Set yourself *three* goals and write them down. They may be new or a mixture of the past left over from the first chapter plus some new goals. Put a date down when you will review your progress. Above all, remember your common sense guide lines.
1. Keep it simple.
2. Practise on the easy ones before tackling the difficult situations or people.
3. Reward yourself for *any* accomplishments.
4. Win a few, lose a few.

To help you with the next stage of development, go back and go through the book again. This time however, don't start at the beginning, go to those chapters which are relevent to your new objectives. Re-read them, and rework the excercises. You may find one particular part very important to you and hang on to it as a "Life-line". Sometimes people go over a certain passage or chapter each day or once a week. If that helps, then do so. Always use anything which helps you.

Until the next time
You have the capability and power within you to learn or relearn all the skills necessary to be an interesting, happy and individual person — *To Be You*.

It takes three things, some willing, some energy, and above all, making friends with yourself. Plenty of people in the world will put you down and dislike you. They don't need any help. Be on *your* side. Be your own best friend.

EXERCISES

Review of Original Goals and New Targets
Original Goals: _____
_____
_____
_____
_____
_____

Rating of success (Scale 1 to 10) _____
Reward for your success _____
_____

New Targets
Goal One _____
_____
_____

Target date _____

Goal Two _____
_____
_____

Target date _____

Goal Three _____
_____
_____

Target date _____

My reward will be _____
_____
_____

REFERENCES

1. Satir, Virginia, *Peoplemaking.* Palo Alto: Science and Behaviour Books, Inc. 1972.
2. Woolams, S., Brown, M. & Huige, K., *Transactional Analysis in Brief*, Ann Arbor: Huron Valley Institute, 1976.
3. Selye, H., *The Stress of Life*, New York: McGraw Hill Book Company, 1976.
4. Bem, S.L., Androgeny vs. The Tight Little Lines of Fluffy Women and Hairy-Chested Men, *Psychology Today*, September 1975, **9**, 58-62.
5. Brandt, A., What it Means to say NO, *Psychology Today*, August 1981, 70-77.
6. Erikson, E., *Childhood and Society*, New York: W.W. Norton, 1950.
7. Sheehy, Gail, *Passages: Predictable Crisis of Adult Life*, New York: Corgi, 1974.
8. Berne, E., *What Do You Say After You Say Hello*, London: Andre Deutsch, 1974.
9. Lankton, S., *Practical Magic; A Translation of Basic Neuro-Linguistic Programming into Clinical Psychotherapy*, Cupertino, CA: Meta Publications, 1980.
10. Schiff, J., et al. *Cathexis Reader: Transactional Analysis Treatment of Psychosis.* New York: Harper & Row, 1975.
11. Smith, M., *When I Say No I Feel Guilty.* New York: Bantam Press, 1975.
12. Ellis, A. & Harper, R.A., *A Guide to Rational Living*, North Hollywood CA: Wilshire Book Co., 1974.
13. Morris, D., *Manwatching*, London: Jonathan Cape, 1977.
14. Bolton, R., *People Skills*, Englewood Cliffs, New Jersey: Prentice-Hall, Inc., 1979.
15. Perenin, M.T. & Jeannerot, M., Subcortical Vision in Man: *Trends in Neuroscience*, Agust, 1979. 2/8, 204-207.
16. Babcock, C. & Keepers, T., *Raising Kids OK*, New York: Grove Press, 1976.
17. Spitz, R., Hospitalization: Genesis of Psychiatric Conditions in Early Childhood, *Psychoanalytic Study of The Child*, 1: 53-74, 1945.
18. Harlow, H.F. & Harrow, M.K., Social Deprivation in Monkeys, *Scientific American*, 207: 136-146, November 1962.
19. Heslin, R., and Collin, J., Personality of the Judge in recognition of Departure from Role Expectation in Social Behaviour and Personality. *Social Behaviour and Personality* Vol. 19, part I 33-36.